THE ULTIMATE

Chocolate

COOKBOOK

THE ULTIMATE Chocolate COOKBOOK

JENNIE REEKIE

WARD LOCK LIMITED · LONDON

Acknowledgements

Food photography   Peter Myers
Home economist   Jackie Burrow
Stylist   Alison Williams

The author and publisher would also like to thank The Glasshouse and
Way-In Living, Harrods for kindly loaning equipment for
photography.

House editor   Susan Dixon
Phototypeset in Linotron Garamond Original by
Tradespools Limited, Frome, Somerset

Printed and bound in Spain by Graficas Reunidas

Contents

NOTES

All spoon measures are level unless otherwise stated.
All eggs used are size 3 unless otherwise stated.
It is important to follow *either* the metric *or* the imperial measures
when using this book. Do *not* use a combination of measures.

Introduction

Few people would dispute that chocolate is the most popular sweet flavour in the Western world. Individual fruits, such as strawberries, raspberries and mangoes may have their devotees, and there may be some who are enslaved by the flavour of almonds or coffee; but nothing is as revered as chocolate. Strong men who spurn all other desserts go into raptures over a chocolate mousse or Black Forest Gâteau, while no self-respecting restaurant would offer less than three chocolate desserts on their sweet trolley.

For some people, their passion for chocolate verges on addiction; they crave for it in the same way that others desire a cigarette, but it is unlikely to be as harmful as smoking unless eaten to excess! There is however, no escaping the fact that chocolate is high in calories, and it must be said that this is not a book for the weight-watcher. But as well as large quantities of fat and carbohydrate, chocolate contains significant amounts of protein, iron and calcium. In fact, when cooking with chocolate, it is not always the chocolate that threatens the waistline, but the cream, sugar and flour that is used with it.

For the most part, chocolate cookery is not the cheapest, simply because the chocolate itself is expensive. It is probably because this basic ingredient is rather a luxury that one tends to use other luxurious ingredients with it such as nuts, fresh cream and alcohol. Chocolate has an affinity not only with rum and brandy, but also with a number of liqueurs including Grand Marnier, Tia Maria and crème de menthe and with those based on coconut.

The result is an array of wonderful concoctions from mousses and soufflés to moist rich cakes, gâteaux and petits fours, and I hope that in the following pages you will be tempted, not only by some of the tried and tested favourites, but by some different and original ways of using this ambrosial ingredient.

Choosing Chocolate for Cooking

There are three main types of chocolate commonly used in cooking – bitter chocolate, chocolate cake covering and plain chocolate, of which plain chocolate is the one most frequently used in this book. White chocolate is not suitable for cooking because it contains no cocoa and, therefore, of course, no colour.

Bitter chocolate, also known as 'baker's chocolate', is unsweetened chocolate especially prepared for cooking. It enables you to achieve a strong chocolate flavour without the end result being too sweet, but I have restricted its use here to just a couple of recipes as it is not very easy to obtain. Any bitter chocolate I did manage to locate was imported, and hence extremely expensive.

If you do find some, and want to experiment, try using it in one of your favourite recipes. It is particularly good in chocolate sauces or for baking – but remember to use slightly less of it than other chocolate and to add a little sugar.

Plain chocolate gives a good strong chocolate flavour. There are a number of different brands available, both British and European; some supermarkets have their own brands as well. Remember though that chocolate quality varies considerably. In order to be called chocolate rather than cake covering, the product must have a minimum of 34 per cent cocoa solids. Some have as much as 47 per cent, so it is worth looking on the back of the pack to check this.

If you prefer a slightly more bitter chocolate, you will find the European brands more to your taste than the British ones. As well as bars of chocolate, you can also buy packets of 'chips'. These have two particularly useful functions: they are good for melting chocolate because the small pieces melt quickly, and the size is perfect for ice creams, biscuits and cookies.

Milk chocolate is rarely used in cooking as it does not give a strong enough chocolate flavour. This can sometimes be an advantage if, for example, you wish to grate a small amount of chocolate over fruit with a delicate flavour. It is, however, used for making Easter eggs, chocolates and chocolate cases, such as the Apricot Fruit Basket on page 72.

Chocolate chips are probably the best thing to buy if milk chocolate is required for anything other than grating, as they are usually cheaper than bars.

Plain and milk chocolate cake covering is often also described as 'cooking chocolate'. This is inaccurate because it does not contain the required minimum of cocoa solids, and has added vegetable and/or coconut oil. In cooking it does not generally produce such a strong flavour as plain chocolate, but it does have advantages for certain dishes. Firstly, it is considerably cheaper, and secondly, it is very much easier to melt than plain chocolate. The coconut oil becomes liquid on heating and this makes a chocolate which is easier to handle than a pure chocolate. Additionally, it avoids the streaky effect sometimes visible after melted plain chocolate has set.

Cocoa is certainly the cheapest, and often the best, way of obtaining a good, strong chocolate flavour, especially when baking. However, it is not used as extensively as plain chocolate for desserts and mousses where a richer flavour is required.

Drinking chocolate can be used to give a more subtle flavour, but as it is very sweet it is almost always necessary to reduce the amount of sugar in the recipe.

Chocolate Tips

MELTING CHOCOLATE

The way in which you melt chocolate is extremely important so as to avoid a solid mass with which you can do nothing.

Break the chocolate into pieces (or use chocolate chips) and put into a basin over a pan of hot, not quite simmering, water (it must *not* be rapidly boiling). If using an electric cooker, turn off the heat once the water has boiled and leave the pan on the ring. Make sure that the basin fits comfortably into the pan so that neither steam nor boiling water get into the basin. As soon as the chocolate has melted, remove from the heat and use as required.

If, you do, however, end up with a solid mass, it is sometimes possible to rectify this by adding a little vegetable oil and beating it well. This works for mousses and similar desserts but not for decorations where it is important for the chocolate to set hard.

Chocolate can also be melted with the addition of vegetable shortening. This makes it more liquid and easier to handle.

If you are only melting a small quantity of chocolate, such as 25 g/ 1 oz, you may find it easier to put the chocolate into a polythene bag, then to seal it and stand the bag in hot, *not* boiling, water. It is important to use a heavy gauge polythene and to ensure that there are no small holes in the bag.

Melting chocolate in a basin in a low oven is an alternative method recommended by some manufacturers.

A microwave oven can also be used for this purpose. Put the chocolate broken into pieces, in a suitable bowl, cover with clingfilm and place in the oven. The exact time it takes to melt the chocolate depends on the quantity, the size of the bowl, etc.

PREPARING CHOCOLATE FOR DIPPING

When using chocolate for dipping, ie for fresh fruit or for chocolates, you may find the chocolate a little easier to use if you add 1 × 15 ml spoon/1 tablespoon vegetable oil or 15 g/½ oz white vegetable shortening to every 175 g/6 oz chocolate.

Melt the chocolate, then pour it into a small jar or glass wide and deep enough for the fruit or chocolate to be dipped into and totally covered.

Hold the ingredient to be dipped with a special dipping fork, fondue fork, skewer or cocktail stick. Dip into the melted chocolate, allow the excess to run off, then remove the dipped ingredient from its fork by pushing it off gently with another fork, skewer or cocktail stick.

MAKING 'BITTER' CHOCOLATE

As unsweetened chocolate is not easy to find, sweetened plain chocolate is generally substituted. Where this is a little too sweet for certain recipes, the chocolate can be made slightly 'bitter' by adding either $1 \times 5\,\text{ml}$ spoon/1 teaspoon instant coffee powder or granules, or a little very strong black coffee. Alternatively, $1 \times 5\,\text{ml}$ spoon/1 teaspoon cocoa powder can be added for every $50\,\text{g}/2\,\text{oz}$ chocolate. This is particularly effective when using chocolate cake covering.

GRATING CHOCOLATE

During hot weather it is best to put the chocolate in a refrigerator for about 30 minutes before grating. If your hands are rather hot, hold the chocolate in a piece of kitchen paper when grating.

CHOPPING CHOCOLATE

This can be done very successfully in a food processor and for many recipes this gives a very good size of chocolate chip. It is not, however, easy to chop chocolate manually, and it is better, in this case, to grate it coarsely.

USING COCOA AND DRINKING CHOCOLATE

When baking, sift cocoa and drinking chocolate with other dry ingredients so that any lumps are removed.

If using cocoa in butter icing, etc, it is important to cook the starch in it, so it should be blended with *very hot* water. (Do not use boiling water as it tends to make a solid lump which is difficult to use).

OTHER POINTS

When using any kind of mould, ensure that it is scrupulously clean so that the chocolate does not stick to the mould and crack. Wash the mould thoroughly in warm water, then dry and polish with a piece of kitchen paper.

Decorations

Chocolate can be used to make a variety of extremely attractive decorations. These can be used on all kinds of cakes, puddings and desserts, quite apart from chocolate ones. For example, cream-topped trifles and pale iced cakes make a perfect foil for the dark appeal of chocolate.

For most decorations the chocolate must be melted and the finished product allowed to set quite hard. This should not be done in a refrigerator or the chocolate will acquire an unattractive chalky 'bloom'. It is best to leave it in the coolest, driest place you have – I put mine, covered, in a shady corner of the garden when the season permits (a kitchen is too warm and steamy to be suitable).

Grated chocolate is the simplest and quickest of decorations, and is very effective. Using a metal grater, and making sure that your hands are cool, grate the chocolate directly on to the food or, if you prefer, on to a plate from where it can be sprinkled with a metal spoon. Do not use your fingers to work with the grated chocolate as the fine particles will melt quickly.

Chocolate curls can be made from plain chocolate or chocolate cake covering; French cooking chocolate is not suitable. Use a thick bar of chocolate – the thicker the block the more successful the results – and make sure it is at the right temperature, ie if it is too cold and hard the chocolate will break; if it is too warm and soft the curls will not hold their shape. Simply scrape a vegetable peeler over the back of the block of chocolate and roll the curls on to a plate. Lift them from the plate with the point of a sharp knife on to the surface to be decorated.

Caraque are long chocolate curls which give a professional and rather glamorous finish to many cakes and gâteaux. Melt the chocolate (page 10) and spread it with a palette knife to less than 0.5 cm / ¼ inch thick over an ungreased surface, preferably a laminated work surface or a sheet of marble. Leave to set in a thin layer. Holding the blade of a knife at an angle of 45°, push away from you and scrape off long curls. Lift them carefully, as they are fragile, using the point of the knife or a skewer; do not discard the small flakes of chocolate that remain on the working surface after you have finished; they can be scattered on top of the cake or dessert in between the pieces of caraque.

Chocolate leaves are made by using real fresh leaves as a mould. The most commonly used leaves are rose leaves because they have a pleasing shape and prominent veining which impresses itself on the chocolate; this makes them easy to work with. Any leaves will do, however, as long as they are not poisonous.

Wash and dry the leaves thoroughly. Dip the underside, which has the most prominent veins, into melted chocolate (page 10) to give a thick and even coating; alternatively, paint with the chocolate. Place on waxed or non-stick silicone paper or greaseproof paper to set. Let the chocolate set completely hard, then carefully peel off the leaf.

Horns are made with the help of cream horn tins. Wash and dry them and shine the inside of the tins with kitchen paper. Pour in some melted chocolate (page 10). Tilt and turn the tin so that the chocolate coats the inside evently; repeat the process to obtain a thicker layer of chocolate (this will be easier to unmould. As you become more proficient, you can make thinner horns.). Leave to set in a cool, dry place. When the chocolate is completely hard, and has begun to shrink away from the inside of the tin, carefully ease out the chocolate horn with the point of a knife.

Chocolate animals are also made by pouring melted chocolate (page 10) into moulds; these are available from good kitchen shops and are the perfect decoration for children's party cakes.

Shapes, patterns and designs can be made in two ways:
(1) Pencil your chosen design lightly on a piece of waxed or non-stick silicone paper. Melt the chocolate (page 10) and pour it into a greaseproof icing bag or nylon piping bag fitted with a small writing pipe. Follow the outline of your drawing first, and fill in the shape afterwards. If you are not making a solid design, but are tracing a trelliswork pattern, for example, make sure that you join up all the threads of chocolate, or the finished design will crack easily when you pick it up after it has set.
(2) Melt the chocolate (page 10) and spread in a thin layer with a palette knife on a piece of waxed or non-stick silicone paper. Leave to set. When the chocolate is hard, but not brittle, use cocktail cutters or a sharp knife to cut out the shapes you want. You can buy cutters in all shapes, from crescents, hearts and bells to butterflies and stars. Simple shapes like squares and triangles can, of course, be cut out with a sharp knife and a steady hand.

Drizzled chocolate is a simple but extremely effective method of decorating cakes, ice cream or biscuits. Simply melt the chocolate in a polythene bag, snip off a corner of the bag and drizzle the chocolate over the food to be decorated.

Making Chocolate Sweetmeats

What present could be more appreciated than a pretty box of home-made chocolate sweetmeats? An old-fashioned term, perhaps, but the great thing is that they are fun to make, and generally much cheaper than bought ones. It is easy to make them look attractive in paper sweet cases, arranged carefully in a box or jar and tied with ribbon. And to end your dinner party in style, impress your guests with a bowl of home-made chocolate-covered mints or scrumptious truffles.

All the recipes here are very straightforward, but once you have mastered them you are sure to go on and experiment with more complicated ideas. While no detailed confectionery knowledge is required, it is, nevertheless, necessary to know how to recognize the different temperatures used when boiling sugar (see chart below). If you progress to making fudge and toffee regularly, it is well worth investing in a sugar thermometer as this is an easy and quick way of checking the temperature.

Sugar Boiling Temperatures

Temperatures	Name of Test	Method of Testing
102–103°C 215–225°F	Thread	Dip the handles of two wooden spoons first into some oil and then into the boiling sugar syrup. The syrup should form into a fine thread when pulled apart.
115°C/240°F	Soft Ball	A little of the syrup can be rolled into a soft ball in your fingers when poured into a cup of cold water.
120°C/250°F	Hard Ball	The mixture forms a larger, harder ball than obtained with the Soft Ball test above.
140°C/280°F	Small Crack	A few drops of the syrup poured into a bowl of cold water soon becomes brittle and a thin piece will snap.
158°C/310°F	Hard Crack	Test as for the Small Crack, but the syrup becomes very brittle.
176°C/345°F	Caramel	The sugar changes to a pale golden-brown and the longer it is boiled, the darker it becomes.

Easter Eggs

Making Easter Eggs at home not only saves money, but provides amusement for all the family, especially for children who will not find it at all difficult, especially if you use chocolate cake covering.

Plastic and metal moulds can be obtained from most good kitchen shops. Make sure they are dry and clean, and polish them well with a piece of kitchen paper before you set to work. Do not grease the moulds. Melt the chocolate (page 10) and spoon some into the mould, tilting it to coat the inside completely. If you have too much, pour it out before it sets; if you have too little, quickly spoon in some more.

Place the mould upside-down on a sheet of greaseproof or waxed paper and leave it in a cold place to set (not a refrigerator). When the first layer of chocolate is hard, you can add another one; this will make the egg easier to unmould, but it is not vital.

When the chocolate is hard and has shrunk away from the edges of the mould a little, ease it out gently with a palette knife.

Fill the Easter egg with sweets and chocolates if you like, and join the two halves by brushing the rims with melted chocolate and pressing them gently together.

Note *Remember that any casualties which break when removed from the mould, can be re-melted and used again.*

Chocolate Dipped Fruits

These provide attractive, quickly made petits fours. A variety of different fruits is suitable, from strawberries and grapes to cherries, peeled lychees and mandarin segments. Choose ripe but firm fruit, free from any blemish. If the fruit has a stalk, such as a cherry, leave it on. Make sure the fruit is clean and dry, and dip each one in melted chocolate (page 10), holding it by the stalk if it has one, otherwise using a cocktail stick. Place on waxed, greaseproof or non-stick paper and leave in a cool place to dry. When the chocolate has set, put the dipped fruit in petits fours cases. Do not store for more than 24 hours; they are at their best up to 12 hours after the chocolate has set.

Rich Chocolate Truffles

100 g/4 oz plain chocolate, broken into small pieces

1 × 15 ml spoon/1 tablespoon liqueur, eg Grand Marnier, Cointreau, Tia Maria, etc

225 g/8 oz icing sugar, sifted

100 g/4 oz unsalted butter

2 × 15 ml spoons/2 tablespoons drinking chocolate

Melt the chocolate (page 10). Remove from the heat and beat in the liqueur, icing sugar and butter until smooth. If necessary, add a little more icing sugar to give a firm paste. Divide into 24 pieces and shape into balls. Roll each one in the drinking chocolate until completely covered, then place in paper sweet cases.

Makes 24

Chocolate Rum Truffles

100 g/4 oz plain chocolate, broken into small pieces

1 × 15 ml spoon/1 tablespoon dark rum

25 g/1 oz unsalted butter

1 egg yolk

100 g/4 oz ground almonds

100 g/4 oz cake crumbs

*50 g/2 oz chocolate **or** coloured vermicelli*

Melt the chocolate with the rum (page 10). Beat in the butter and egg yolk, then remove from the heat. Stir in the ground almonds and cake crumbs to make a smooth firm paste. Divide into 24 pieces and shape into balls. Roll in the vermicelli until completely covered, then place in paper sweet cases.

Makes 24

Chocolate Cream Truffles

100 g/4 oz milk chocolate, broken into pieces

4 × 15 ml spoons/4 tablespoons double cream

½ × 2.5 ml spoon/¼ teaspoon vanilla essence

275 g/10 oz icing sugar, sifted

2 × 15 ml spoons/2 tablespoons extra icing sugar

½ × 2.5 ml spoon/¼ teaspoon ground cinnamon

Melt the chocolate (page 10), then stir in the cream and vanilla essence. Remove from the heat and gradually beat in 275 g/10 oz of the icing sugar to give a firm paste. Divide into 24 pieces and shape into balls.

Sift the remaining icing sugar with the cinnamon on to a sheet of greaseproof paper. Roll the truffles in the spiced sugar until completely coated, then place in paper sweet cases.

Makes 24

ABOVE   Making chocolate leaves (page 13)
ABOVE RIGHT   Making chocolate horns
(page 13)
RIGHT   Making caraque (page 12)

Mint Crisps

4 × 15 ml spoons/4 tablespoons water
4 × 15 ml spoons/4 tablespoons granulated sugar
1 × 5 ml spoon/1 teaspoon peppermint essence
225 g/8 oz plain chocolate, broken into small pieces

Well butter a piece of greaseproof paper. Put the water and sugar into a small, heavy-based pan. Stir over low heat until the sugar has dissolved, then boil rapidly to 140°C/280°F on a sugar thermometer (small crack stage). Remove from the heat and stir in the essence. Pour evenly over the greaseproof paper and leave to set. When the mixture is quite firm, either break up into small pieces with a rolling-pin or chop finely in a food processor; the pieces should resemble coarse breadcrumbs.

Melt the chocolate (page 10), then remove from the heat and stir in the peppermint pieces. Put teaspoonfuls of the mixture on sheets of buttered greaseproof or waxed paper, spread into circles about 2.5 cm/1 inch in diameter, and leave to set.

Makes about 30

Chocolate Peppermint Creams

The creams look particularly attractive in a box if half are green and half are white.

1 size 1 egg white
½ × 2.5 ml spoon/¼ teaspoon peppermint essence
a few drops green food colouring (optional)
350 g/12 oz icing sugar, sifted
100 g/4 oz plain or milk chocolate, broken into small pieces

Put the egg white, essence and colouring, if used, in a mixing bowl and beat lightly. Beat in the icing sugar gradually to make a firm paste (the exact amount of sugar will depend on the size of the egg). Place on a surface lightly dusted with icing sugar and knead until smooth. Roll out, using icing sugar to prevent it from sticking, to a thickness of about 0.75 cm/¼ inch. Stamp out circles, using a 4 cm/1½ inch cutter and place on a baking sheet lined with greaseproof paper. Mark each one with the prongs of a fork. Leave in a warm place overnight to dry out.

Melt the chocolate (page 10). Dip each peppermint cream in the chocolate so that only half is coated. Shake off any excess chocolate and place on buttered greaseproof paper or foil. Leave to set.

Makes about 48

A Selection of Sweetmeats
Chocolate Dipped Fruit (page 15), Colettes (page 20), Chocolate Peppermint Creams, Walnut Mocha Fudge (page 23), Easter Eggs (page 15), Chocolate Cream Truffles (page 16) **and** *Fruit and Nut Clusters (page 22)*

Colettes

225 g / 8 oz plain chocolate, broken into
small pieces

4 × 15 ml spoons / 4 tablespoons water

1 × 15 ml spoon / 1 tablespoon strong
black coffee

50 g / 2 oz butter

2 egg yolks

1 × 5 ml spoon / 1 teaspoon dark rum

Melt 100 g / 4 oz of the chocolate (page 10). Remove from the heat and put a good teaspoonful into 18 waxed paper sweet cases. Using the handle of a teaspoon, spread evenly round the base and sides of each case. Leave to set in a cool place.

Put the remaining chocolate into a small pan with the water and coffee. Stir over very low heat until the chocolate has melted, then boil for 2 minutes, stirring frequently. Remove the pan from the heat and allow the mixture to cool. Beat in the butter, a little at a time, then blend in the egg yolks and the rum. Leave in a cold place until thickened.

When the chocolate cases have set, peel off the paper sweet cases carefully. Spoon the filling into a piping bag fitted with a 1.25 cm / ½ inch rose nozzle and pipe into each chocolate case.

Makes 18

Chocolate Whirls

A recipe producing very rich, smooth chocolates.

50 g / 2 oz soft brown sugar

2 egg yolks

150 ml / ¼ pint single cream

200 g / 7 oz plain chocolate, broken into
small pieces

Put the sugar and egg yolks in a mixing bowl over a pan of hot, not boiling, water. Whisk together until pale and thick. Blend in the cream and continue to cook, stirring until the custard coats the back of a spoon. Turn off the heat, but leave the basin over the pan of water. Add the chocolate, and stir until it has melted. Cover and leave to cool until the mixture is of a piping consistency. Spoon into a piping bag fitted with a large star nozzle and pipe in whirls into paper sweet cases. Leave to set.

Makes 18

Note *If the mixture is left to set before being piped, it should be reheated over a pan of hot water.*

Stuffed Dates

These are quite deliciously rich, and, although you can make them with dried dates, they really are better made with fresh, as these are not quite so sweet.
In addition to being served as chocolates or petits fours, these dates are also excellent dipped into whipped cream.

450 g / 1 lb fresh dates
75 g / 3 oz plain chocolate, broken into small pieces
50 g / 2 oz butter
1 × 15 ml spoon / 1 tablespoon ground almonds
1 egg yolk
*1 × 15 ml spoon / 1 tablespoon Grand Marnier **or** other orange liqueur*
grated rind of 1 small orange

COATING

175 g / 6 oz plain chocolate, broken into small pieces
15 g / ½ oz vegetable shortening

Using a sharp knife, make a slit down the side of each date and remove the stone. Pull off the hard remains of the stalk. Melt the chocolate (page 10) and remove from the heat. Cream the butter. Beat in the ground almonds, then the egg yolk. Beat in the Grand Marnier, orange rind and finally the chocolate. Mix well, then chill in a refrigerator for about 10 minutes, or until the mixture is firm enough to pipe.

Fill a small piping bag fitted with a small plain nozzle about 0.75 cm / ¼ inch wide with the mixture, or put it into a heavy-gauge polythene bag, work it down to one corner and snip off the corner with scissors. Holding the dates between the thumb and forefinger, press them open and pipe the filling into the centre. Chill in a refrigerator for about 15 minutes.

To make the coating, melt the chocolate with the vegetable shortening (page 10), and pour into a narrow deep glass or cup. Taking one date at a time, skewer one end with a cocktail stick and dip into the melted chocolate. Allow the excess chocolate to drip off, then place on a piece of foil and use a second stick to push the date off the dipping stick. Leave to set.

Makes about 24

VARIATION *Fill the dates with half of the mixture and then pipe the remainder on to some buttered greaseproof paper, making small 'blobs' the size of a large marble. Chill for about 15 minutes, then dip into melted chocolate and leave to set.*

Fruit and Nut Clusters

100 g / 4 oz plain chocolate, broken into small pieces

2 × 15 ml spoons / 2 tablespoons clear honey

100 g / 4 oz mixed dried fruit

*50 g / 2 oz nuts, chopped, eg almonds, hazelnuts **or** brazils*

grated rind of ½ orange

DECORATION
glacé cherries

Melt the chocolate with the honey (page 10). Stir in the dried fruit, nuts and orange rind until well coated in the chocolate. Drop teaspoonfuls of the mixture on to buttered greaseproof or waxed paper, or into paper sweet cases. Press a small piece of glacé cherry on the top of each cluster and leave to set.

Makes 24–28

VARIATION *Use milk chocolate instead of plain chocolate.*

Different coloured glacé cherries look very attractive.

Chocolate Toffee

450 g / 1 lb granulated sugar

100 g / 4 oz butter

150 ml / ¼ pint water

½ × 2.5 ml spoon / ¼ teaspoon cream of tartar (optional)

*100 g / 4 oz plain chocolate **or** chocolate cake covering, broken into small pieces*

Butter a shallow 17.5 cm / 7 inch square cake tin. Put the sugar, butter, water and cream of tartar, if using, in a large pan. Stir over low heat until the sugar has dissolved. Bring to the boil and cook without stirring to 140°C / 280°F on a sugar thermometer (small crack stage). After 120°C / 250°F is reached (hard ball stage), reduce the heat and cook very slowly up to the required temperature. Remove from the heat and add the chocolate. Stir gently until melted, then pour immediately into the prepared tin. When beginning to set, mark into squares with a sharp knife. Leave to set, and cut into squares when cold.

Makes 36

Note *These toffees can be wrapped individually in waxed papers for storing.*

Chocolate and Orange Fudge

This makes a soft, smooth, creamy fudge.

450 g / 1 lb granulated sugar
150 ml / ¼ pint milk
100 g / 4 oz plain chocolate cake covering, broken into small pieces
100 g / 4 oz butter
grated rind and juice of 1 orange

Well butter a shallow 17.5 cm/7 inch square tin. Put all the ingredients in a large pan, and stir over low heat until the sugar has dissolved. Bring to the boil and boil rapidly to 115°C/240°F on a sugar thermometer, (soft ball stage). Stir from time to time to prevent it from burning. Remove from the heat and leave to cool for about 3 minutes. Beat rapidly until thick and creamy. Pour immediately into the prepared tin. When it is beginning to set, mark the fudge into squares with a sharp knife. When cold, cut into squares.

Makes 36

Walnut Mocha Fudge

This makes a firm, crunchy fudge.

450 g / 1 lb soft brown sugar
175 g / 6 oz canned evaporated milk
150 ml / ¼ pint water
50 g / 2 oz butter
1 × 15 ml spoon / 1 tablespoon instant coffee granules
100 g / 4 oz plain chocolate **or** chocolate cake covering, broken into small pieces
100 g / 4 oz walnuts, chopped

Well butter a shallow 17.5 cm/7 inch square tin. Put the sugar, milk, water, butter and coffee in a large pan. Stir over low heat until the sugar has dissolved. Bring to the boil and boil rapidly to 115°C/240°F on a sugar thermometer (soft ball stage). Stir from time to time to prevent it from burning. Remove from the heat and stir in the chocolate until melted. Add the walnuts, and beat until the mixture is thick and creamy. Pour immediately into the prepared tin. When it is beginning to set, mark into squares with a sharp knife. When cold, cut into squares.

Makes 36

Large Cakes and Gâteaux

No matter whether they are plain, Victoria-sandwich cakes, rich, moist dark cakes or gâteaux filled with thick whipped cream and fruit, chocolate cakes are supreme. Most are made with cocoa, some with drinking chocolate and others with melted chocolate. The methods of making them are varied, too, which is why a chocolate cake is never just another cake – each one is quite different.

There is also a wide choice of fillings and toppings ranging between whipped cream, simple butter icing made with either cocoa or melted chocolate, rich Continental butter creams, fudgy frostings and rich, thick glacé icings. The possible variations are innumerable, and all of them mouthwatering.

A number of the gâteaux in this chapter could be served as a dessert rather than with morning coffee or afternoon tea. If you think I have omitted some of your favourites, look for it either in the Cold Desserts or Chocolate Classics chapters – I hope you'll find it there.

Simple Cake

This very easily made cake is perfect as a base for a children's birthday cake. Turn it into a maypole by putting a stick in the centre with some streamers coming from it, or decorate it with sweets spelling the child's name.

200 g / 7 oz self-raising flour
25 g / 1 oz cocoa powder
a pinch of salt
225 g / 8 oz caster sugar
100 g / 4 oz butter **or** margarine
175 g / 6 oz canned evaporated milk
2 eggs
2 × 15 ml spoons / 2 tablespoons water
1 × 5 ml spoon / 1 teaspoon vanilla essence

FILLING AND TOPPING

225 g / 8 oz icing sugar
40 g / 1½ oz drinking chocolate
65 g / 2½ oz butter

Grease and line two 19–20 cm / 7½–8 inch sandwich tins. Sift together the flour, cocoa, salt and sugar into a large bowl. Melt the butter or margarine in a pan. Take 3 × 15 ml spoons / 3 tablespoons of the evaporated milk and put into a small pan for the icing. Put to one side. Beat the eggs with the remaining evaporated milk, water and vanilla essence. Make a well in the centre of the dry ingredients, add the egg mixture together with the melted fat, and beat well until blended.

Divide the mixture between the prepared tins and bake in a moderate oven, 180°C / 350°F / Gas 4, for 20–25 minutes or until the cakes spring back when pressed lightly. Allow to cool in the tins for a few minutes, then turn out on to a wire rack and leave to cool.

To make the filling, sift the icing sugar and drinking chocolate into a basin. Put the butter into the pan with the reserved milk, and heat gently until the butter has melted. Pour over the icing sugar mixture and beat until well blended. Put to one side for about 10 minutes until the mixture begins to thicken. Use some of the mixture to sandwich the cakes together, and spread the remaining icing over the top and sides. Decorate as liked.

Economical Chocolate Cake

This is an old war-time recipe of my mother's; it makes a very good, plain cake.

50 g / 2 oz softened margarine
100 g / 4 oz caster sugar
1 egg, beaten
175 g / 6 oz plain flour
a pinch of salt
2 × 5 ml spoons / 2 teaspoons baking powder
1 × 15 ml spoon / 1 tablespoon cocoa powder
4 × 15 ml spoons / 4 tablespoons milk

ICING
50 g / 2 oz margarine
1 × 15 ml spoon / 1 tablespoon cocoa powder
275 g / 10 oz icing sugar, sifted
2 × 15 ml spoons / 2 tablespoons hot water

Grease and line a 17.5 cm / 7 inch cake tin. Cream the margarine, add the sugar and continue to beat until the mixture is light and fluffy. Beat in the egg, a little at a time. Sift together the flour, salt, baking powder and cocoa and fold into the creamed mixture, alternately with the milk.

Turn the mixture into the prepared tin and bake in a moderate oven, 180°C / 350°F / Gas 4, for about 50 minutes, or until the top springs back when pressed lightly. Allow to cool in the tin for 5 minutes, then turn out on to a wire rack and leave to cool. When the cake is quite cold, split into two rounds.

To make the icing, put the margarine and cocoa into a small pan over low heat until the margarine has melted. Remove from the heat and beat in about a third of the icing sugar, then beat in a little of the hot water and the remaining icing sugar alternately. Beat well until the mixture begins to thicken. Spread evenly over both rounds, and swirl the icing up on the top of the cake with a round-bladed knife or fork to make an attractive pattern. Sandwich the rounds together. Leave to set for at least 15 minutes.

Note *It is particularly important that the margarine is very soft.*

Moist Chocolate Cake

A perfect recipe when time is of the essence. Once baked, this really good moist cake can be completed in minutes.

275 g/10 oz soft brown sugar
25 g/1 oz cocoa powder
150 ml/¼ pint water
225 g/8 oz plain flour
2 × 5 ml spoons/2 teaspoons baking powder
1 × 2.5 ml spoon/½ teaspoon
bicarbonate of soda
1 × 2.5 ml spoon/½ teaspoon salt
100 g/4 oz butter
1 × 5 ml spoon/1 teaspoon vanilla essence
2 eggs, separated
150 ml/¼ pint soured cream

FILLING AND DECORATION
4 × 15 ml spoons/4 tablespoons chocolate
and hazelnut spread
icing sugar

Grease and line two 20 cm/8 inch sandwich tins. Put 75 g/3 oz of the sugar into a pan with the cocoa and water. Stir over low heat until the sugar has dissolved, then bring to the boil and simmer gently for 2 minutes. Remove from the heat and allow to cool. Sift together the flour with the baking powder, bicarbonate of soda and salt. Cream the remaining sugar and the butter until light and fluffy. Add the vanilla essence and beat in the egg yolks, one at a time. Fold in the dry ingredients alternately with, first, the cooled chocolate and then the soured cream. Whisk the egg whites until stiff and fold gently into the mixture.

Turn the mixture into the prepared tins and bake in a moderate oven, 180°C/350°F/Gas 4, for about 45 minutes or until the cakes spring back when pressed lightly. Allow to cool in the tins for 2 minutes, then turn out on to a wire rack and leave to cool.

When cold, sandwich the cakes together with the chocolate and hazelnut spread. Dust the top with icing sugar.

Wholemeal Chocolate Cake

175 g/6 oz butter

175 g/6 oz light soft brown sugar

2 × 15 ml spoons/2 tablespoons molasses

3 eggs, beaten

115 g/4½ oz wholemeal flour

40 g/1½ oz cocoa powder

2 × 5 ml spoons/2 teaspoons baking powder

2 × 15 ml spoons/2 tablespoons milk

ICING AND DECORATION

100 g/4 oz butter

125 g/5 oz soft brown sugar

5 × 15 ml spoons/5 tablespoons water

25 g/1 oz cocoa powder

6 walnut halves

Grease and line a 20 cm/8 inch cake tin. Cream together the butter, sugar and molasses until pale in colour. Beat in the eggs, a little at a time, adding 1 × 15 ml spoon/1 tablespoon of the flour with the last amount of egg. Sift in the cocoa powder and baking powder, and fold in gently. Fold in the remaining flour and finally fold in the milk.

Turn the mixture into the prepared tin and bake in a moderate oven, 180°C/350°F/Gas 4, for 1 hour or until the top springs back when pressed. Remove from the oven, turn out on to a wire rack and leave to cool. When cold, split the cake into two rounds.

To make the icing, put all the ingredients, apart from the walnuts, into a pan and stir over low heat until the sugar has dissolved. Boil rapidly for 2 minutes. Remove from the heat, and allow to cool slightly, stirring frequently. Spread 2 × 15 ml spoons/ 2 tablespoons of the icing over the bottom round of cake. Sandwich the two cake rounds together. When the icing is the consistency of single cream, pour the remainder over the cake to coat the top and sides. Decorate with the walnut halves and leave to set.

Chocolate and Orange Cake

225 g/8 oz self-raising flour

75 g/3 oz cocoa powder

225 g/8 oz unsalted butter

275 g/10 oz caster sugar

2 eggs, beaten

250 ml/8 fl oz buttermilk

FILLING AND ICING

225 g/8 oz unsalted butter

grated rind of 1 orange

225 g/8 oz icing sugar, sifted

juice of ½ orange

DECORATION

fresh orange segments

Grease and line two 20–22.5 cm/8–9 inch sandwich tins. Sift together the flour and cocoa. Cream the butter and sugar until light and fluffy, then gradually beat in the eggs. Stir in the buttermilk. Fold in the flour and cocoa.

Turn the mixture into the prepared tins and bake in a moderate oven, 180°C/350°F/Gas 4, for about 40 minutes. Remove from the oven and allow to cool in the tins for 5 minutes. Turn out on to a wire rack and leave to cool. When cold, split each cake into two layers.

To make the icing, cream the butter with the orange rind until soft. Gradually beat in the icing sugar, alternately with the orange juice. Use some of the butter icing to sandwich the cakes together. Spread the remaining butter icing over the top and sides of the cake, and mark with a fork. Decorate the top of the cake with the orange segments.

Loganberry Cake

4 eggs, separated

100 g/4 oz caster sugar

25 g/1 oz cocoa powder

50 g/2 oz fresh white breadcrumbs

100 g/4 oz ground almonds

FILLING AND TOPPING

150 ml/¼ pint double cream

about 4 × 15 ml spoons/4 tablespoons loganberry jam **or** conserve

DECORATION (optional)

a few fresh loganberries **or** raspberries

Grease and line a 20 cm/8 inch cake tin. Whisk the egg yolks and sugar until thick and creamy. Sift in the cocoa powder and fold in with the breadcrumbs. Whisk the egg whites until stiff, then fold half into the mixture. Fold in the almonds, then the remainder of the egg whites, taking care to lose as little air as possible.

Turn the mixture into the prepared tin and bake in a moderate oven, 180°C/350°F/Gas 4, for 45 minutes. Remove from the oven and allow to cool.

When the cake is quite cold, carefully split in half. Whip the cream until stiff, and fill the centre of the cake with half the cream and the loganberry jam or conserve. Pipe the remaining cream over the top and decorate with fresh loganberries or raspberries, if liked.

Rum Cake

This moist chocolate cake should be served with lashings of whipped cream or Crème Chantilly (see page 108). It is best if kept for at least 24 hours before serving so that it becomes very soft and moist. Once cut, it should be eaten as soon as possible.

100 g/4 oz self-raising flour
1 × 2.5 ml spoon/½ teaspoon bicarbonate of soda
40 g/1½ oz cocoa powder
3 × 15 ml spoons/3 tablespoons dark rum
6 × 15 ml spoons/6 tablespoons cold water
100 g/4 oz butter
225 g/8 oz caster sugar
2 eggs, beaten
50 g/2 oz ground almonds

Grease and line a 19–20 cm/7½–8 inch round cake tin. Sift together the flour and bicarbonate of soda. Sift the cocoa into a basin and stir in the rum and water. Cream the butter and sugar until light and fluffy. Gradually beat in the eggs, a little at a time. Fold in the ground almonds gently, then the flour and cocoa mixture alternately.

Turn the mixture into the prepared tin and bake in a warm oven, 160°C/325°F/Gas 3, for about 1 hour or until the cake springs back when pressed lightly. Allow to cool in the tin for 5 minutes, then turn out on to a wire rack and leave to cool. Wrap in greaseproof paper and foil, or store in an airtight tin until required.

Tipsy Cake

When short of time I have made this with a bought chocolate sponge cake and, whilst obviously not quite as good as a home-made sponge, it passes very well.

75 g/3 oz self-raising flour

25 g/1 oz cocoa powder

4 eggs

100 g/4 oz caster sugar

3 × 15 ml spoons/3 tablespoons corn oil

SYRUP

175 g/6 oz granulated sugar

2 × 15 ml spoons/2 tablespoons instant coffee granules

450 ml/¾ pint water

3 × 15 ml spoons/3 tablespoons brandy **or** dark rum

300 ml/½ pint whipping cream

DECORATION

coffee beans

Grease and line a 20 cm/8 inch cake tin. Sift together the flour and cocoa powder. Whisk the eggs and sugar until thick and creamy, and the whisk leaves a trail when lifted out of the mixture. Fold in the flour and cocoa, then fold in the corn oil very carefully.

Turn the mixture into the prepared tin and bake in a moderate oven, 180°C/350°F/Gas 4, for 45 minutes. Remove from the oven and allow to cool in the tin for 5 minutes, then turn out on to a wire rack and leave to cool.

To make the syrup, put the sugar and coffee in the water in a small pan and stir over low heat until the sugar has dissolved. Bring to the boil. Remove from the heat and add the brandy or the rum.

Place the cake on a serving dish and prick all over with a skewer. Pour over a little of the hot coffee syrup and allow it to soak in. Pour over a little more and continue doing this until all the syrup has been absorbed. Leave to stand for at least 2 hours.

Whip the cream until thick but not stiff and spread it all over the top and sides of the cake. Swirl into a pattern with a fork. Decorate with a few coffee beans.

Chocolate and Chestnut Log

This rather unusual method of making a whisked sponge produces a beautifully light cake.

25 g/1 oz plain flour

25 g/1 oz cornflour

1½ × 15 ml spoons/1½ tablespoons cocoa powder

1 × 5 ml spoon/1 teaspoon baking powder

3 eggs

1 egg white

125 g/5 oz caster sugar

FILLING AND TOPPING

400 g/14 oz canned unsweetened chestnut purée

50 g/2 oz soft brown sugar

2 × 15 ml spoons/2 tablespoons dark rum

50 g/2 oz plain chocolate

150 ml/¼ pint double cream

3 × 15 ml spoons/3 tablespoons single cream

Sift together the flour, cornflour, cocoa and baking powder. Whisk the eggs together with the extra egg white, in a large mixing bowl. Whisk in the sugar, 1 × 15 ml spoon/1 tablespoon at a time. Continue to whisk until the mixture is the consistency of very lightly whipped cream. Whisk in the sifted ingredients, 1 × 15 ml spoon/1 tablespoon at a time; whisk well after each addition.

Turn the mixture into the prepared tin, and spread evenly. Bake in a moderately hot oven, 200°C/400°F/Gas 6, for about 12 minutes or until the cake springs back when pressed lightly. Turn out on to a piece of greaseproof or non-stick silicone paper, dredged with icing or caster sugar. Carefully peel off the lining paper, trim off the edges, and roll up the Swiss roll, keeping the paper inside the roll. Put to one side and allow to cool.

To make the filling, beat the chestnut purée with the brown sugar and rum to give a soft spreading consistency. Grate the chocolate coarsely or form into curls with a vegetable peeler (page 12). Whip the double and single creams together.

Unroll the Swiss roll, and spread with 3 × 15 ml spoons/3 tablespoons of the cream, then the chestnut purée mixture. Sprinkle with half the grated chocolate or chocolate curls, reserving the best ones for decoration. Re-roll the Swiss roll and place on a serving dish. Spread the remaining cream over the top and sides of the cake, and decorate with the remaining grated chocolate or chocolate curls.

Caribbean Gâteau

4 eggs, separated

175 g / 6 oz caster sugar

4 × 15 ml spoons / 4 tablespoons very hot water (see **Note**)

75 g / 3 oz plain flour

25 g / 1 oz cocoa powder

1½ × 5 ml spoons / 1½ teaspoons baking powder

FILLING AND DECORATION

400 g / 14 oz canned mangoes

300 ml / ½ pint whipping cream

2 chocolate flake bars, crumbled

Grease and line a 20 cm / 8 inch round cake tin. Whisk the egg yolks with the sugar until thick and creamy. Gradually whisk in the very hot water. Whisk until thick and creamy, and the whisk leaves a trail when lifted out of the mixture. Sift in the flour, cocoa and baking powder, and fold in. Whisk the egg whites until stiff, then fold gently into the mixture.

Turn the mixture into the prepared tin and bake in a moderate oven, 180°C/350°F/Gas 4, for about 50 minutes, or until the cake springs back when pressed lightly. Allow to cool in the tin for 5 minutes, then turn out on to a wire rack and leave to cool. When cold, split the cake into three rounds.

To make the filling, drain the mangoes, reserving the syrup. Set aside about three of the best mango slices for decoration and chop the remainder. Whip the cream lightly with 2 × 15 ml spoons / 2 tablespoons of the mango syrup.

Spread the bottom round of the cake with a third of the cream, half the chopped mango pieces and a third of the chocolate flake. Place the next layer of cake on top, and spread with another third of the cream, the mangoes and chocolate flake. Top with the last round of cake, and spread with the last of the cream. Decorate with the reserved mango slices and the remainder of the chocolate flake.

Note *It is particularly important that the water is not actually boiling. A kettle with boiling water left for a few minutes, once boiled, will be the right temperature.*

Pear and Chocolate Gâteau

75 g/3 oz self-raising flour

25 g/1 oz cocoa powder

4 eggs

100 g/4 oz caster sugar

FILLING AND TOPPING

100 g/4 oz plain chocolate, broken
into pieces

2 egg yolks

150 ml/¼ pint whipping cream

2 ripe pears

1 × 15 ml spoon/1 tablespoon lemon juice

Make the filling first. Melt the chocolate (page 10). Remove from the heat and beat in the egg yolks, one at a time. Beat in 1 × 15 ml spoon/1 tablespoon of the cream. Whip the remainder of the cream, then fold into the chocolate mixture. Chill for 1 hour.

Grease and line two 21–22.5 cm/8½–9 inch sandwich tins. Sift together the flour and cocoa. Whisk the eggs and sugar until thick and creamy, and the whisk leaves a trail when lifted out of the mixture. Fold in the flour.

Turn the mixture into the prepared tins. Bake in a moderately hot oven, 190°C/375°F/Gas 5, for 15–20 minutes, or until well risen and the cakes spring back when pressed lightly. Allow to cool in the tins for 5 minutes, then turn out on to a wire rack and leave to cool.

Peel the pears and slice them thinly. Dip in the lemon juice to preserve the colour. When the cakes are quite cold, spread one of them with half the chocolate filling. Cover with two-thirds of the pears, and place the second cake on top. Spread with the last of the chocolate mixture and arrange the remaining pears on top.

Caribbean Gâteau (page 33)
OVERLEAF LEFT   Loganberry Cake (page 29)
*OVERLEAF RIGHT   Peppermint Caterpillar
(page 43)*

Honey Cake

This cake can either be eaten warm as a pudding or cold as a cake; it is particularly good for picnics and packed lunches.

225 g/8 oz honey

225 g/8 oz caster sugar

50 g/2 oz butter

150 ml/¼ pint light ale

1 egg, beaten

350 g/12 oz plain flour

2 × 5 ml spoons/2 teaspoons baking powder

3 × 5 ml spoons/3 teaspoons ground allspice

100 g/4 oz ground almonds

ICING AND DECORATION

50 g/2 oz plain chocolate, broken into pieces

2 × 15 ml spoons/2 tablespoons hot water

25 g/1 oz butter

100 g/4 oz icing sugar

1½ × 15 ml spoons/1½ tablespoons cocoa powder

4 × 15 ml spoons/4 tablespoons apricot jam, sieved

50 g/2 oz blanched split almonds

Grease and line a 32.5 × 22.5 cm/13 × 9 inch Swiss roll tin. Put the honey, sugar, butter and light ale in a large pan. Stir over low heat until the butter has melted and the sugar dissolved. Remove from the heat and allow to cool. Whisk the egg into the mixture. Sift together the flour, baking powder and allspice, then beat gradually into the melted ingredients. Stir in the almonds.

Turn the mixture into the prepared tin and spread evenly. Bake in a moderately hot oven, 190°C/375°F/Gas 5, for about 20 minutes or until firm. Remove from the oven, turn out of the tin on to a wire rack (the cake should be iced while it is still warm).

To make the icing, melt the chocolate with the water and butter (page 10), then remove from the heat. Sift in the icing sugar and cocoa and beat well. Replace the basin over the hot water to keep the icing warm. Warm the apricot jam in a small pan. Spread evenly over the top of the cake, then spread with the icing. Arrange the split almonds on the top of the cake, then cut into squares. Serve warm, or leave to cool, and store in an airtight tin.

Large and Small Cakes and Biscuits
Spice Cake (page 41), Chocolate and Orange Cake (page 29). Chocolate Ginger Squares (page 46), Florentines (page 99), Shortbread Zig-Zags (page 52), Chocolate Meringues (page 47) **and** *Apple Cake (page 40)*

Apple Cake

3 cooking apples, preferably Bramleys
juice of ½ lemon
2 eggs
200 g / 7 oz caster sugar
100 g / 4 oz butter
150 ml / ¼ pint milk
175 g / 6 oz plain chocolate cake covering,
broken into pieces
200 g / 7 oz plain flour
3 × 5 ml spoons / 3 teaspoons baking powder

Grease and flour a 20 × 30 cm/8 × 12 inch roasting tin. Peel, core and slice the apples thinly. Put in a bowl of cold water with the lemon juice and put to one side. Whisk the eggs with 175 g/6 oz of the sugar until thick and creamy, and the whisk leaves a trail when lifted out of the mixture.

Put the butter, milk and chocolate into a pan. Heat gently until the butter and chocolate have melted, then bring to the boil. While still boiling, pour the mixture over the eggs and sugar and stir until well blended. Sift in the flour and baking powder, and fold in carefully.

Turn the mixture into the prepared tin. Drain and dry the apple slices, and arrange them evenly over the top of the mixture (this is important – too much apple in the centre and the edges will burn before the centre has cooked). Sprinkle with the remaining sugar and bake in a moderately hot oven, 200°C/ 400°F/Gas 6, for about 30 minutes. Serve warm with cream, or cool in the tin, and serve sliced.

Fudgy Date Cake

175 g / 6 oz butter
100 g / 4 oz soft brown sugar
2 × 15 ml spoons / 2 tablespoons golden syrup
3 eggs, beaten
200 g / 7 oz self-raising flour, sifted
75 g / 3 oz dried dates, chopped
100 g / 4 oz plain chocolate, grated coarsely
or chopped finely

Grease and line a 22.5 cm/9 inch deep sandwich tin. Cream together the butter, sugar and syrup until light and fluffy. Beat in the eggs gradually, adding 1 × 15 ml/1 tablespoon of the flour with the last amount of egg. Fold in the remainder of the flour, then fold in the dates and chocolate.

Turn the mixture into the prepared tin and bake in a moderate oven, 180°C/350°F/Gas 4, for about 45 minutes. Turn out on to a wire rack and leave to cool.

Banana and Walnut Cake

175 g/6 oz butter

100 g/4 oz caster sugar

3 eggs, beaten

175 g/6 oz self-raising flour

50 g/2 oz drinking chocolate

50 g/2 oz walnuts, chopped finely

FILLING AND DECORATION

150 ml/¼ pint double cream

2 × 15 ml spoons/2 tablespoons milk

2 bananas

1 × 15 ml spoon/1 tablespoon lemon juice

25 g/1 oz icing sugar, sifted

extra icing sugar

Grease and line two 17.5 cm/7 inch sandwich tins. Cream the butter and sugar together until light and fluffy. Gradually beat in the eggs, a little at a time, adding 1 × 15 ml spoon/1 tablespoon of the flour with the last amount of egg. Sift in the remaining flour and drinking chocolate, and fold into the mixture. Fold in the walnuts.

Turn the mixture into the prepared tins and bake in a moderately hot oven, 190°C/375°F/Gas 5, for about 25 minutes. Remove from the oven and allow to cool in the tins for a couple of minutes, then turn out on to a wire rack and leave to cool.

To make the filling, whip the cream with the milk until it is just stiff. Slice the bananas and toss in the lemon juice. Fold into the cream with the icing sugar. Sandwich the cakes together with the banana cream and dust with icing sugar before serving.

Spice Cake

The mashed potato in this cake helps to keep it very moist.

175 g/6 oz butter

350 g/12 oz caster sugar

4 eggs, separated

50 g/2 oz plain chocolate, broken into pieces

225 g/8 oz mashed potato

250 g/9 oz plain flour

1 × 2.5 ml spoon/½ teaspoon
bicarbonate of soda

2 × 5 ml spoons/2 teaspoons baking powder

1 × 2.5 ml spoon/½ teaspoon salt

1 × 5 ml spoon/1 teaspoon ground cinnamon

1 × 2.5 ml spoon/½ teaspoon
ground nutmeg

1 × 2.5 ml spoon/½ teaspoon ground cloves

150 ml/¼ pint milk

Grease and flour a 1.2 kg/3 lb loaf tin. Cream the butter and sugar until light and fluffy, then beat in the egg yolks. Melt the chocolate (page 10). If the potatoes are cold, heat in a non-stick pan until lukewarm (any hotter and they will melt the butter). Beat the chocolate into the butter and sugar, then beat in the potatoes. Sift the flour with the bicarbonate of soda, baking powder, salt and spices. Fold into the mixture alternately with the milk. Whisk the egg whites until stiff, then fold gently into the mixture.

Turn the mixture into the prepared tin and bake in a moderate oven, 180°C/350°F/Gas 4, for about 1¼ hours or until a skewer inserted into the centre comes out clean. Allow to cool in the tin for 5 minutes, then turn out on to a wire rack and leave to cool. Serve sliced.

Butterfly Cake

This is the perfect recipe for anyone daunted by the thought of making novelty cakes. Although the instructions may seem complicated, it is, in fact, a very easy cake to make.

200 g / 7 oz self-raising flour
2 × 5 ml spoons / 2 teaspoons baking powder
25 g / 1 oz cocoa powder
225 g / 8 oz soft margarine
225 g / 8 oz caster sugar
grated rind of 1 large orange
4 eggs, beaten

BUTTER ICING

175 g / 6 oz butter
275 g / 10 oz icing sugar, sifted
2 × 15 ml spoons / 2 tablespoons orange juice

GLACÉ ICING

500 g / 1 lb 2 oz icing sugar
75 g / 3 oz drinking chocolate
cold water

TO ASSEMBLE

2 chocolate flake bars
30 cm / 12 inch square cake board
2 liquorice 'pipes'

Grease and line a 22.5 cm/9 inch square cake tin. Sift together the flour, baking powder and cocoa into a mixing bowl. Add all the remaining ingredients, and beat well for about 2 minutes.

Turn the mixture into the prepared tin and bake in a warm oven, 160°C/325°F/Gas 3, for about 1 hour 5 minutes, or until well risen and golden-brown. Allow to cool in the tin for 5 minutes, then turn out on to a wire rack and leave to cool.

To make the butter icing, cream the butter and beat in half the icing sugar. Gradually beat in the remainder of the icing sugar and the orange juice alternately. Split the cake into three layers. Spread the butter icing on each layer and sandwich together. To shape the butterfly's 'wings', lay the cake on a board and cut in half diagonally, then trim off about 2.5 cm/1 inch from the corner opposite each diagonal cut. Place the two 'wings' on a wire rack with a tray underneath.

To make the glacé icing, sift 450 g/1 lb icing sugar with the drinking chocolate into a bowl. Gradually beat in enough cold water (about 7 × 15 ml spoons/ 7 tablespoons) to give a thick, smooth, coating consistency. Sift the remaining icing sugar into a separate bowl and stir in just enough cold water to give a thick icing for piping. Put into a small greaseproof or nylon icing bag with a writing pipe.

Pour the glacé icing over the two 'wings' and spread it evenly to coat the top and sides. While this icing is still wet, pipe lines about 2 cm/¾ inch apart, parallel to the straight sides of the cake on the top. Quickly draw a skewer or the point of a knife through the icing at right angles to the piping, first in one direction and then in the other, about 2 cm/¾ inch apart, wiping the knife or skewer between each line.

Trim about 2.5 cm/1 inch off the chocolate flakes, then sandwich together with a little glacé icing (use any that has run off the cake on to the tray beneath). Spread a narrow strip of icing down the centre of the cake board, the length of the flakes, and place them, one on top of the other, on top to form the body. While they are still wet, carefully lift the 'wings' off the rack using two fish slices, and place them in position on the board. Cover the ends of the liquorice pipes with a little icing and place in position for the antennae. Leave to set for at least 2 hours.

Peppermint Caterpillar

3 eggs

75 g / 3 oz caster sugar

65 g / 2½ oz self-raising flour

2 × 15 ml spoons / 2 tablespoons
cocoa powder

FILLING AND DECORATION

350 g / 12 oz butter

550 g / 1¼ lb icing sugar, sifted

peppermint essence

a little green colouring

25 g / 1 oz plain chocolate, broken into small
pieces

Grease and line a 32.5 × 22.5 cm / 13 × 9 inch Swiss roll tin. Place a paper cake case, about 5–7.5 cm / 2–3 inches wide, on a baking tray. Whisk the eggs and sugar until thick and creamy, and the whisk leaves a trail when lifted out of the mixture. Sift in the flour and cocoa, and fold in.

Put 1 heaped 15 ml spoon / 1 heaped tablespoon of the mixture into the paper cake case and turn the remainder of the cake mixture into the prepared tin. Spread evenly. Bake both cakes in a moderately hot oven, 200°C / 400°F / Gas 6, for about 10 minutes or until the cake springs back when pressed lightly. Remove both the Swiss roll and the small individual cake from the oven. Turn the Swiss roll on to a piece of greaseproof or non-stick silicone paper, dredged with icing or caster sugar. Carefully peel off the lining paper, trim off the edges and quickly roll up the Swiss roll lengthways, (ie to make a long thin, rather than a short fat, roll), keeping the paper inside the roll. Allow to cool. Cool the small cake.

To make the filling, cream the butter, beat in the icing sugar, then beat in the peppermint essence and colouring. Unroll the Swiss roll, spread with one-third of the filling and re-roll. Taper one end of the roll to make the caterpillar's tail by shaving off a little of the cake from either side. Peel off the case of the small cake and spread its base with a little of the remaining filling. Place on the fatter end of the roll to make the caterpillar's head. Spread all but 3 × 15 ml spoons / 3 tablespoons of the icing over the cakes.

Melt the chocolate (page 10) and cool slightly. Beat into the remaining icing, then put into a greaseproof or nylon icing bag fitted with a writing pipe. Pipe lines across the Swiss roll to make segments for the caterpillar's body, and pipe in eyes and a mouth. Leave to set.

Refrigerator Biscuit Cake

I was given this recipe in the 1960s by the late James Robertson Justice's mother who had served it to members of the Royal Family when they had lunched with her in Scotland.

100 g / 4 oz plain chocolate, broken into small pieces.

175 g / 6 oz unsalted butter

3 egg yolks

75 g / 3 oz lump sugar

6 × 15 ml spoons / 6 tablespoons water

1 × 15 ml spoon / 1 tablespoon granulated sugar

150 ml / 1/4 pint warm strong black coffee

2 × 15 ml spoons / 2 tablespoons dark rum

32 Nice biscuits

DECORATION
chocolate vermicelli

Melt the chocolate (page 10). Remove from the heat and allow to cool slightly. Cream the butter until light and fluffy, then beat in the chocolate.

In a separate basin, whisk the egg yolks lightly. Put the lump sugar and water into a small, heavy-based pan and stir over low heat until the sugar has dissolved. Boil rapidly to 103°C/225°F on a sugar thermometer (thread stage). Whisk into the egg yolks gradually until the mixture has a mousse-like consistency. Add to the butter mixture, a little at a time, and beat well.

Dissolve the granulated sugar in the coffee and add the rum. Quickly dip eight biscuits into the coffee syrup and place flat on a plate in two rows. Spread with a little of the chocolate butter icing. Repeat these layers twice more, then finish with a layer of biscuits. Spread the remaining chocolate butter icing over the top and sides, and sprinkle with chocolate vermicelli. Chill in a refrigerator for 2 hours or until quite firm.

Small Cakes, Biscuits and Cookies

Although one can buy any number of excellent biscuits and cookies, there is nothing quite like home-made biscuits in the tin. In fact, I try not to make them too often as they are so more-ish and the temptation to have one with a cup of tea or coffee becomes too great. However, if you are strong-willed or do not have to watch your weight, they are a great standby, as most of them keep well in an airtight tin, or can be frozen and do not take long to defrost.

As well as making the recipes I have given here, you may like to try coating one side of any of your favourite bought biscuits with chocolate. This is a good way for young children to do some 'cooking' without using the oven and generally making havoc. Melt some chocolate cake covering for them and let them spread it on bought biscuits; they will keep quietly busy for ages, even if they do get a bit sticky!

As I prefer moist, rich chocolate cakes I have not included many small cakes; these have a tendency to dryness and can be very fiddly to ice and decorate. An exception is Cherry Fingers (page 48), which count among my favourite cakes. They have the essential qualities of moistness and richness, are made with drinking chocolate and ground almonds, and have an unusual filling of cream cheese and cherry jam.

A useful idea for a quick, delicious and sustaining snack is to put one or two pieces of chocolate – preferably French plain cooking chocolate – into a chunk of very fresh French bread. This is perfect for picnics, long car journeys and other occasions when you need something to keep you going but do not have the facilities for elaborate preparations. I first had a 'chocolate sandwich' like this when I was a child in France on an exchange visit. Most of the adults had gone to visit an elderly relative and we had been left to amuse ourselves in the village. This is what we had for tea, and I have never forgotten it.

Chocolate Ginger Squares

125 g / 5 oz plain flour
25 g / 1 oz cocoa powder
1 × 2.5 ml spoon / ½ teaspoon salt
2 × 5 ml spoons / 2 teaspoons baking powder
125 g / 5 oz light soft brown sugar
2 eggs, separated
6 × 15 ml spoons / 6 tablespoons corn oil
6 × 15 ml spoons / 6 tablespoons milk
25 g / 1 oz crystallized ginger, chopped finely

ICING
25 g / 1 oz butter
25 g / 1 oz cocoa powder
3 × 15 ml spoons / 3 tablespoons hot water
225 g / 8 oz icing sugar, sifted
25 g / 1 oz crystallized ginger, chopped finely

Grease and line a 17.5 cm/7 inch square cake tin. Sift together the flour, cocoa, salt and baking powder into a bowl. Add the sugar. Blend the egg yolks, oil and milk. Pour into the centre of the dry ingredients and beat well. Mix in the ginger. Whisk the egg whites until stiff, then fold gently into the mixture.

Turn the mixture into the prepared tin and bake in a moderate oven, 180°C/350°F/Gas 4, for about 45 minutes, or until well risen and firm. Remove from the oven, allow to cool in the tin for 5 minutes, then turn out on to a wire rack and leave to cool.

To make the icing, melt the butter in a pan. Blend the cocoa with the hot, not boiling, water, then pour into the icing sugar. Add the butter and beat well to give a thick glossy icing (use a little extra water if necessary). Add the ginger and beat well. Pour evenly over the top of the cake. Leave to set. Cut into squares to serve.

Makes 9

Crunchy Date Wedges

225 g / 8 oz digestive biscuits
100 g / 4 oz butter
3 × 15 ml spoons / 3 tablespoons
Demerara sugar
225 g / 8 oz dried dates, chopped
50 g / 2 oz raisins
100 g / 4 oz plain chocolate or chocolate cake covering, broken into pieces

Lightly butter a 22.5 cm/9 inch sandwich tin. Put the digestive biscuits in a polythene bag and crush with a rolling-pin, or use a food processor. Heat the butter and sugar gently in a pan until the butter has melted and the sugar dissolved. Remove from the heat and add the dates and raisins. Stir in the biscuit crumbs and blend well.

Spread the mixture evenly over the base of the prepared tin and press down firmly. Melt the chocolate (page 10) and spread over the biscuit mixture. Mark out wedges with a sharp knife while the chocolate is still slightly soft. Leave to set for at least 1 hour. Cut into wedges to serve.

Makes 10

Chocolate Meringues

These meringues look very attractive on a serving dish mixed with plain meringues.
Alternatively, sandwich one plain and one chocolate meringue together.

3 egg whites
75 g / 3 oz caster sugar
75 g / 3 oz icing sugar
25 g / 1 oz cocoa powder
150 ml / ¼ pint whipping cream (optional)

Lightly oil a baking tray and line with non-stick silicone paper. Whisk the egg whites until they form stiff peaks. Gradually whisk in the caster sugar, 1 × 5 ml spoon / 1 teaspoon at a time until the mixture is stiff and shiny. Sift together the icing sugar and cocoa and fold into the mixture.

Either put the mixture in a piping bag fitted with a large rose nozzle, and pipe 12 meringues on to the prepared baking tray, or put 12 heaped spoonfuls of the mixture on to the baking tray. Bake in a very cool oven, 120°C/250°F/Gas ½, for 1 hour. Reduce the heat as much as possible and cook for a further 4 hours, or until the meringues are quite dry. Remove from the oven and allow to cool. For serving, whip the cream lightly, if used, and sandwich the meringues together, two at a time, with the cream.

Makes 6

Coconut Meringue Slices

*100 g / 4 oz butter **or** margarine*
225 g / 8 oz plain flour, sifted
cold water
*200 g / 7 oz plain chocolate cake covering, grated coarsely **or** chopped finely*
2 egg whites
100 g / 4 oz caster sugar
100 g / 4 oz desiccated coconut

Rub the fat into the flour until the mixture resembles fine breadcrumbs. Bind with cold water to form a firm dough. Roll out on a floured surface and use to line the base and sides of a 17.5 × 27.5 cm / 7 × 11 inch Swiss roll tin. Sprinkle the chocolate over the pastry. Whisk the egg whites until they form stiff peaks, then whisk in half the sugar, 1 × 5 ml spoon / 1 teaspoon at a time until the mixture is stiff and shiny. Fold in the remaining sugar and the coconut. Spoon it over the chocolate and spread evenly, using a palette knife, until completely covered.

Bake in a moderate oven, 180°C/350°F/Gas 4, for 30 minutes. Remove from the oven and allow to cool slightly. Cut into slices while still warm.

Makes 14

Cherry Fingers

175 g/6 oz butter

175 g/6 oz caster sugar

4 eggs, separated

a pinch of salt

125 g/5 oz drinking chocolate

50 g/2 oz ground almonds

25 g/1 oz plain flour, sifted

FILLING AND DECORATION

50 g/2 oz butter

50 g/2 oz cream cheese

50 g/2 oz icing sugar, sifted

4 × 15 ml spoons/4 tablespoons
good quality black cherry jam

extra icing sugar

Grease and line a 32.5 × 22.5 cm/13 × 9 inch Swiss roll tin. Cream the butter and sugar until light and fluffy. Beat in the egg yolks with the salt, one at a time. Sift in the drinking chocolate, and fold in. Fold in the ground almonds and flour. Whisk the egg whites until stiff, then fold in gently, a third at a time (the mixture may look curdled at this stage, but this does not matter).

Turn the mixture into the prepared tin and spread evenly. Bake in a moderate oven, 180°C/350°F/Gas 4, for about 25 minutes. Turn out on to a sheet of greaseproof paper on a wire tray. Peel off the lining paper carefully. Leave to cool, then cut the cake in half to make two squares.

To make the filling, cream the butter with the cream cheese and icing sugar. Spread over one of the squares of cake. Spread the cherry jam on top and sandwich the cakes together. Cut in half, then cut each half into eight fingers. Dust with icing sugar before serving.

Makes 16

Chocolate and Almond Slices

200 g / 7 oz plain flour
1 × 5 ml spoon / 1 teaspoon baking powder
25 g / 1 oz cocoa powder
100 g / 4 oz butter
100 g / 4 oz soft brown sugar
2 × 15 ml spoons / 2 tablespoons golden syrup
a little milk
25 g / 1 oz flaked almonds

Well butter a 27.5 × 17.5 cm / 11 × 7 inch Swiss roll tin. Sift together the flour, baking powder and cocoa. Cream the butter and sugar until light and fluffy, then beat in the syrup. Gradually work in the dry ingredients to make a smooth dough.

Press into the prepared tin and prick all over with a fork. Brush with a little milk and sprinkle with the almonds. Bake in a moderate oven, 180°C/350°F/ Gas 4, for about 30 minutes or until golden-brown, then cool in the tin and mark into fingers while still warm.

Makes 18

Mixed Nut Slice

75 g / 3 oz butter
25 g / 1 oz caster sugar
1 egg yolk
1 × 2.5 ml spoon / ½ teaspoon vanilla essence
100 g / 4 oz plain flour
1 × 15 ml spoon / 1 tablespoon cocoa powder

FILLING
2 eggs
100 g / 4 oz soft brown sugar
75 g / 3 oz chopped mixed nuts
75 g / 3 oz desiccated coconut

TOPPING
2 × 15 ml spoons / 2 tablespoons chopped mixed nuts
2 × 15 ml spoons / 2 tablespoons desiccated coconut
*75 g / 3 oz plain **or** milk chocolate cake covering, broken into pieces*

Butter a 17.25 cm × 27.5 cm / 7 × 11 inch Swiss roll tin. Cream the butter and sugar until light and fluffy, then beat in the egg yolk and vanilla essence. Sift in the flour and cocoa and form into a stiff dough. Turn on to a lightly floured surface and knead lightly. Roll out to a rectangle a little smaller than the tin, then lift into the tin and press into the edges.

To make the filling, whisk the eggs and sugar until thick and creamy, and the whisk leaves a trail when lifted out of the mixture. Fold in the nuts and coconut, then spread evenly over the chocolate base. Sprinkle with the nuts and coconut for the topping.

Bake in a moderately hot oven, 190°C/375°F/Gas 5 for 20–25 minutes or until golden-brown. Remove from the oven and allow to cool in the tin. When cold, cut into 15 squares.

Melt the cake covering and drizzle over the nut slices (page 13). Leave to set.

Makes 15

Chocolate Croissants

1 × 5 ml spoon/1 teaspoon sugar
*100 ml/3 fl oz **plus** 1 tablespoon warm water*
2 × 5 ml spoons/2 teaspoons dried yeast
225 g/8 oz strong plain flour
1 × 5 ml spoon/1 teaspoon salt
15 g/½ oz lard
25 g/1 oz caster sugar
1 egg, lightly beaten
75 g/3 oz butter
50 g/2 oz milk chocolate chips
1 egg

EGG WASH
1 × 15 ml spoon/1 tablespoon water
1 × 2.5 ml spoon/½ teaspoon caster sugar

Dissolve the sugar in the water in a basin, sprinkle with the yeast and leave in a warm place for 10 minutes or until frothy. Sift together the flour and salt, rub in the lard and mix in the sugar. Make a well in the centre of the flour, pour in the yeast liquid and the egg, and mix to a soft dough. Turn on to a lightly floured surface and knead well for about 5 minutes. When the dough feels smooth and elastic, roll it out to a rectangle about 30 × 12.5 cm/12 × 5 inches.

Divide the butter into three. Dot the top two-thirds of the dough with one part of the butter, cut into small pieces. Fold the bottom third up and the top third down, like an envelope. Seal the edges, give the dough a half turn, then roll out again and repeat this process with the remaining two parts of butter. Fold the dough, put into an oiled polythene bag and chill for at least 1 hour.

Roll out to a 30 cm/12 inch square, cover with a piece of oiled clingfilm and leave for 10–15 minutes. Trim the edges, divide into four squares, then divide each of these into two triangles.

To make the egg wash, beat the egg with the water and sugar. Brush all over the dough, then sprinkle with the chocolate chips. Roll each triangle up loosely, starting from the wide side and going towards the point.

Place the croissants on oiled baking sheets, with the tip underneath, and curve into crescents. Brush again with the egg wash and cover with oiled clingfilm. Put in a warm place and leave until the dough has doubled in size, then remove the clingfilm, brush again with the egg wash and bake in a hot oven, 220°C/425°F/Gas 7 for 15–20 minutes or until well risen and golden-brown. Remove from the oven and cool on a wire rack.

Makes 8

Chocolate Chip Cookies

I really like the texture of these biscuits – the outside edges become very crisp while the centre stays deliciously soft.

100 g/4 oz butter
100 g/4 oz caster sugar
1 egg, beaten
1 × 2.5 ml spoon/½ teaspoon vanilla essence
125 g/5 oz wholemeal flour
a pinch of salt
3 × 15 ml spoons/3 tablespoons milk
100 g/4 oz plain chocolate chips

Well grease three or four large baking sheets. Cream the butter and sugar until light and fluffy. Beat in the egg and vanilla essence gradually. Sift in the flour and salt, and fold in with the milk and chocolate chips.

Put spoonfuls of the mixture on to the prepared baking sheets, spacing them well apart. Bake in a moderate oven, 180°C/350°F/Gas 4, for about 12–15 minutes or until golden-brown. Leave to cool on the baking trays for 1 minute, then remove with a palette knife and cool on a wire rack.

Makes about 36

Chocolate Chip Shortbread

100 g/4 oz plain flour
50 g/2 oz cornflour
50 g/2 oz caster sugar
100 g/4 oz butter
25 g/1 oz milk chocolate chips

Sift together the flour and cornflour. Add the sugar, then rub in the butter. The mixture will become crumbly at first, but continue working it until it clings together in heavy lumps. Turn on to a board or working surface dusted with flour or cornflour and knead lightly. Place the ball on a buttered baking tray and roll out to make a 22.5 cm/9 inch circle. Prick the surface with a fork. Mark out 10 portions with a sharp knife and flute the edges with your fingers. Sprinkle with the chocolate chips.

Bake in a warm oven, 160°C/325°F/Gas 3, for 30–35 minutes or until the shortbread is cooked; but it should not be browned. Remove from the oven and leave to cool on the baking tray for 10 minutes, then, using a fish slice, lift carefully on to a wire rack to cool.

Makes 10

Pineapple Shortbreads

125 g / 5 oz plain flour
75 g / 3 oz drinking chocolate
a pinch of salt
100 g / 4 oz butter
150 ml / ¼ pint double cream
225 g / 8 oz canned pineapple rings, drained

Sift together the flour, drinking chocolate and salt. Rub in the butter until the mixture is crumbly, then knead together until smooth. Roll out on a floured surface and cut into eight 10 cm / 4 inch diameter circles.

Put the shortbreads on to greased baking trays and bake in a warm oven, 160°C / 325°F / Gas 3, for about 15 minutes. Remove from the oven and allow to cool on the tray for 5 minutes. Transfer to a wire rack and leave to cool. Whip the cream until stiff, and divide between the biscuits. Cut the pineapple rings into quarters and place two pieces on each biscuit.

Makes 8

Shortbread Zig-Zags

125 g / 5 oz plain flour
50 g / 2 oz caster sugar
100 g / 4 oz butter
1 × 15 ml spoon / 1 tablespoon cocoa powder
1 × 15 ml spoon / 1 tablespoon
drinking chocolate

Well butter a 17.5 cm / 7 inch square cake tin. Sift all but 15 g / ½ oz of the flour into a bowl. Add the sugar, then rub in the butter until the mixture is crumbly. Divide the mixture in half. Work in the remaining flour to one half and the cocoa and drinking chocolate to the other. Turn on to a board or working surface lightly dusted with flour, and knead each dough separately until smooth. Roll out and cut into strips 3.75 cm / 1½ inches wide. Put these strips diagonally across the tin; any trimming can be cut into shapes and baked on a baking tray.

Bake in a warm oven, 160°C / 325°F / Gas 3, for about 30–35 minutes, or until crisp but not brown (trimmings will only take about 5 minutes). Remove from the oven, mark out into fingers and leave to cool in the tin.

Makes 12

Chocolate Biscuit Squares

A very popular recipe of my mother's, who makes these endlessly.

175 g/6 oz rich tea biscuits
100 g/4 oz butter
75 g/3 oz golden syrup
25 g/1 oz cocoa powder
50 g/2 oz seedless raisins
50 g/2 oz glacé cherries, chopped finely
25 g/1 oz blanched almonds, chopped
25 chocolate buttons

Grease a shallow 17.5 cm/7 inch square cake tin. Put the biscuits in a polythene bag and crush with a rolling-pin, or use a food processor. Heat the butter, syrup and cocoa gently until the fat has melted. Remove from the heat and stir in first the raisins, cherries and almonds and then the biscuit crumbs. Stir until thoroughly mixed.

Press the mixture into the prepared tin and space the chocolate buttons evenly on top in lines of five. Leave in a cool place to set, then cut into squares, between the buttons.

Makes 25

Chocolate Sandwich Biscuits

100 g/4 oz butter
100 g/4 oz caster sugar
2 × 15 ml spoons/2 tablespoons beaten egg
1 × 2.5 ml spoon/½ teaspoon vanilla essence
225 g/8 oz plain flour, sifted

FILLING
75 g/3 oz butter
175 g/6 oz soft brown sugar
100 g/4 oz plain chocolate cake covering, broken into pieces

Cream together the butter and sugar until pale and creamy. Beat in the egg and vanilla essence, a little at a time, alternating with some of the flour. Stir in the remaining flour to give a firm dough. Knead the dough until smooth, then roll out on a floured surface to a thickness of about 0.5 cm/¼ inch. Stamp out circles with a 5 cm/2 inch fluted cutter.

Place the circles on greased baking trays and prick with a fork. Re-roll the trimmings and cut out more biscuits. Bake in a moderate oven, 180°C/350°F/Gas 4, for about 15 minutes until golden. Leave on the trays to harden for a few minutes, then remove to a wire rack and allow to cool.

To make the filling, beat together the butter and sugar until pale and creamy. Melt the chocolate (page 10). Beat into the creamed mixture, then leave to thicken slightly. Sandwich the biscuits together two at a time, with some of the chocolate icing.

Makes about 20

Hot Puddings

Hot puddings must be amongst the most nostalgic foods for all of us, recalling to memory favourite meals of childhood days. But some hot puddings, such as hot chocolate soufflé, are nothing if not sophisticated.

It can be difficult to get the timing of these dishes right, especially if you are entertaining and do not want to be in the kitchen just before serving the meal. Steamed puddings should be prepared well in advance as they take a long time to cook. Soufflés too can be prepared ahead if you put them in a *cold* oven and increase the cooking time accordingly. You can make up the soufflé up to 24 hours in advance and keep it in a refrigerator. To cook, put it in a cold oven, then set the oven to the required temperature. As it heats up, so will the soufflé, which will rise slowly. If a cold soufflé mixture is put into a hot oven, a seal is quickly formed over the top of it, preventing the soufflé from rising.

Most hot chocolate puddings are improved if served with pouring or spooning cream, lightly whipped double cream – sweetened if liked – ice cream or a hot chocolate sauce.

Steamed Chocolate Pudding with Orange Sauce (page 63)
OVERLEAF LEFT Marbled Savarin (page 80)
OVERLEAF RIGHT Tia Maria Soufflé (page 79)
***and** Avocado Fool (page 73)*

Hot Chocolate Soufflé

100 g/4 oz plain chocolate, broken
into pieces

2 × 15 ml spoons/2 tablespoons
water **or** liqueur

100 g/4 oz caster sugar

4 eggs, separated

icing sugar

Butter a 1.2 litre/2 pint soufflé dish. Melt the chocolate with the water or liqueur (page 10). Whisk together the sugar and egg yolks until thick and pale. Beat in the melted chocolate until well blended. Whisk the egg whites until stiff, then fold very gently into the chocolate mixture.

Pour the mixture into the prepared soufflé dish and bake in a moderately hot oven, 190°C/375°F/Gas 5, for about 30 minutes until well risen and firm, but slightly wobbly. Dust the top with icing sugar and serve at once.

Serves 4

Note *An extra egg white will make the soufflé even lighter.*

Hot Cocoa and Orange Soufflé

25 g/1 oz butter **or** margarine

25 g/1 oz plain flour, sifted

150 ml/¼ pint milk

25 g/1 oz cocoa powder

75 g/3 oz caster sugar

grated rind and juice of 1 orange

4 eggs, separated

icing sugar

Butter a 1.5 litre/2½ pint soufflé dish. Melt the fat in a pan and stir in the flour. Add the milk and bring to the boil, stirring until thick and smooth. Add the cocoa, sugar and grated orange rind and juice. Return to the boil, stirring until well blended, then remove from the heat and leave to cool. Add the egg yolks, one at a time, beating until smooth. Whisk the egg whites until stiff, then fold gently into the chocolate sauce.

Pour the mixture into the prepared soufflé dish. Bake in a moderate oven, 180°C/350°F/Gas 4, for about 45 minutes until well risen and firm, but slightly wobbly. Dust the top with icing sugar and serve at once.

Serves 4

Strawberry Chocolate Box (page 70)

Chocolate Soufflé Flan

175 g / 6 oz plain flour
a pinch of salt
75 g / 3 oz butter
cold water

FILLING
2 eggs, separated
25 g / 1 oz caster sugar
1 × 15 ml spoon / 1 tablespoon cornflour
300 ml / ½ pint half cream
100 g / 4 oz plain chocolate, grated coarsely

Sift together the flour and salt, and rub in the butter until the mixture resembles fine breadcrumbs. Bind together with cold water to make a firm dough. Turn on to a floured surface and knead lightly until smooth. Roll out and use to line a 20 cm / 8 inch flan tin or dish. Bake blind in a moderately hot oven, 190°C/375°F/Gas 5, for 20 minutes.

To make the filling, mix together the egg yolks, sugar and cornflour. Whisk in the cream, then stir in the chocolate, and blend well. Whisk the egg whites until they form stiff peaks. Fold gently into the mixture, then turn into the baked flan case. Bake at 190°C/375°F/Gas 5 for 25–35 minutes or until the mixture is well risen and golden-brown. Serve with cream.

Serves 6

Baked Pears

150 ml / ¼ pint water
50 g / 2 oz sugar
1 vanilla pod
6 large pears, peeled, cored and quartered
100 g / 4 oz chocolate, broken into pieces
25 g / 1 oz butter

Butter an ovenproof dish. Put the water, sugar and vanilla pod into a pan over low heat and stir until the sugar has dissolved. Bring to the boil. Add the pears and poach gently for 10 minutes.

Melt the chocolate with the butter (page 10). Stir in 2 × 15 ml spoons / 2 tablespoons of the juice from the pan. Drain the pears, discarding the vanilla pod, and place in the prepared dish. Pour over the melted chocolate, cover and bake in a moderate oven, 180°C/350°F/Gas 4, for 15 minutes. Serve with ice cream or cream.

Serves 4–6

Baked Hazelnut and Cherry Pudding

50 g / 2 oz hazelnuts
175 g / 6 oz butter **or** margarine
175 g / 6 oz light soft brown sugar
3 eggs
125 g / 5 oz self-raising flour
25 g / 1 oz cocoa powder
450 g / 1 lb frozen pitted black cherries, thawed and drained **or** 450 g / 1 lb canned pitted black cherries, drained but reserving 4 × 15 ml spoons / 4 tablespoons syrup

Well butter an ovenproof dish approximately 20 × 22.5 cm/8 × 9 inches in diameter. Chop the hazelnuts very finely, or grind in a blender or food processor until they resemble coarse breadcrumbs. Cream the fat and the sugar until light and fluffy. Beat in the eggs, a little at a time, adding 1 × 15 ml spoon/1 tablespoon of the flour with the last amount of egg. Sift together the flour and cocoa and fold in alternately with the cherries, syrup if used, and the nuts.

Turn the mixture into the prepared dish and bake in a moderate oven, 180°C/350°F/Gas 4, for about 45 minutes until well risen and firm to the touch. Turn out and serve with whipped cream.

Serves 6

Chocolate Eve's Pudding

This combination of blackcurrant and chocolate quite transforms this standard pudding.

350 g / 12 oz fresh **or** frozen blackcurrants, thawed
75 g / 3 oz Demerara sugar
100 g / 4 oz butter **or** margarine
100 g / 4 oz caster sugar
2 eggs, beaten
75 g / 3 oz self-raising flour
25 g / 1 oz cocoa powder

Butter an ovenproof dish approximately 17.5–20 cm/7–8 inches in diameter. Put in the blackcurrants and sprinkle with the sugar. Cream the fat and the sugar until light and fluffy. Beat in the eggs, a little at a time, adding 1 × 15 ml spoon/1 tablespoon of the flour with the last amount of egg. Sift in the flour and cocoa and fold into the mixture.

Spoon the mixture over the fruit and spread evenly. Bake in a moderate oven, 180°C/350°F/Gas 4, for about 40 minutes. Serve with cream.

Serves 4–6

Saucy Sponge Pudding

Do not be alarmed by the rather strange way in which this pudding is made! During cooking, the cake mixture rises above the cocoa/water and sugar mixture to give a light sponge on top with a rich chocolate sauce underneath.

75 g/3 oz self-raising flour
25 g/1 oz cocoa powder
a pinch of salt
1 × 5 ml spoon/1 teaspoon baking powder
100 g/4 oz soft margarine
100 g/4 oz soft brown sugar
2 eggs
1 × 2.5 ml spoon/½ teaspoon vanilla essence
1 × 15 ml spoon/1 tablespoon milk

SAUCE

100 g/4 oz soft brown sugar
25 g/1 oz cocoa powder
300 ml/½ pint hot water

Well butter a 1.2 litre/2 pint ovenproof dish. Sift together the flour, cocoa, salt and baking powder into a mixing bowl. Add the margarine and sugar. Beat the eggs with the vanilla essence and milk, add to the remaining ingredients and beat well for 2 minutes until thoroughly mixed. Spoon into the prepared dish.

To make the sauce, blend together the sugar and cocoa, then gradually stir in the water, and mix well. Pour over the sponge mixture. Bake in a moderately hot oven, 190°C/375°F/Gas 5, for 30–40 minutes. Serve with cream.

Serves 4–6

Sussex Pudding

225 g/8 oz self-raising flour
1 × 2.5 ml spoon/½ teaspoon salt
75 g/3 oz shredded suet
150 ml/¼ pint water (approx)
100 g/4 oz butter, preferably unsalted
25 g/1 oz soft brown sugar
50 g/2 oz drinking chocolate

Well butter a 1.2 litre/2 pint pudding basin. Sift together the flour and salt. Add the suet, then bind with the water to make a soft, but not sticky, dough. Roll out to a 20 cm/8 inch circle and use to line the prepared basin.

Cream the butter, then beat in the sugar and drinking chocolate. Form into a ball and put in the middle of the basin. Dampen the edges of the pastry, then fold over and press together, so that the chocolate ball is completely enclosed. Cover with a double layer of buttered greaseproof paper or with foil, and steam for 2½–3 hours (add more water to the pan if necessary). Turn out and serve with cream.

Serves 4–6

Steamed Chocolate Pudding with Orange Sauce

The light mousse-like orange sauce makes all the difference to this fairly basic steamed pudding.

1 medium-sized orange
175 g/6 oz butter
175 g/6 oz caster sugar
3 eggs, beaten
125 g/5 oz self-raising flour
25 g/1 oz cocoa powder

SAUCE

25 g/1 oz butter, preferably unsalted
grated rind and juice of 1 orange
2 × 5 ml spoons/2 teaspoons flour
50 g/2 oz caster sugar
1 egg, separated

DECORATION (optional)

orange rind, pared

Well butter a 1.2 litre/2 pint pudding basin. Thinly pare the orange rind, then cut into matchstick pieces. Cream together the butter, sugar and orange shreds until the mixture is light and fluffy. Beat in the eggs, a little at a time, adding 1 × 15 ml spoon/1 tablespoon of flour with the last amount of egg. Sift in the remaining flour and the cocoa and fold into the mixture.

Turn the mixture into the prepared basin, cover with a double piece of buttered greaseproof paper or with foil, and steam for 1¾–2 hours (add more water to the pan if necessary). Turn out of the basin and serve with the orange sauce and orange rind, if used.

To make the sauce, cream the butter with the orange rind and gradually beat in the flour mixed with the sugar, then add the egg yolk. Make the orange juice up to 150 ml/¼ pint with water, and beat into the mixture; it does not matter if the mixture looks curdled at this stage. Turn the mixture into a small, heavy-based pan and cook over low heat, stirring all the time, until the sauce thickens. Cover the pan with foil and put to one side until ready to serve, then re-heat gently. Whisk the egg white until stiff and fold gently into the sauce just before serving.

Serves 6

VARIATION *Add 2 × 15 ml spoons/2 tablespoons Cointreau or Grand Marnier to the sauce in place of 2 × 15 ml spoons/2 tablespoons water.*

Rich Chocolate Fondue

Chocolate fondue must be one of the greatest delights for real chocoholics, so I have deliberately chosen a really rich one here.

What you choose to dip into your fondue is entirely a matter of personal preference, and although diced squares of cake, sponge fingers etc, (which may be more suitable for children) can be used, I personally prefer fresh fruit. Cubes of pineapple, whole fresh strawberries, slices of apples, peaches and pears, orange segments etc, are all delicious dipped into the fondue.

225 g / 8 oz plain chocolate, broken
into pieces

150 ml / 1/4 pint double cream

1 1/2 × 15 ml spoons / 1 1/2 tablespoons rum,
brandy **or** liqueur, eg Tia Maria, Grand
Marnier **or** Cointreau

40 g / 1 1/2 oz blanched almonds,
finely chopped

FOR DIPPING

900 g / 2 lb prepared fresh fruit (see above)

Place the chocolate in a fondue pan with the cream, and heat very gently, stirring until the chocolate has melted. Stir in the rum, brandy or liqueur and the nuts, then stand over a very gentle flame on a fondue stand.

Use fondue forks to skewer the fruit to dip into the fondue, and serve with crisp biscuits or wafers and whipped cream, if liked.

Serves 6

Milk Chocolate Fondue

200 g / 7 oz milk chocolate cake covering,
broken into pieces

grated rind of 1 orange

150 ml / 1/4 pint single cream

FOR DIPPING

900 g / 2 lb prepared fresh **or** canned fruit **or**
sponge finger biscuits **or** squares of sponge
cake (see previous recipe)

Place the chocolate in a fondue pan with the orange rind and cream, and heat very gently, stirring until the chocolate has melted. Remove from the heat and place over a very gentle flame on a fondue stand.

Use fondue forks to skewer the fruit, cake or biscuits.

Serves 6

Cold Desserts and Ices

Many people, who would not think twice about enjoying a variety of fruit fillings in a box of chocolates, have surprisingly conservative ideas about teaming up chocolate with different fruits for desserts. However, there are few fruits that chocolate does not accompany successfully, unless it has such a delicate flavour that the chocolate completely overpowers it. I have, therefore, deliberately tried to include as wide a variety of fruit as possible.

For me, the finest of all cold chocolate desserts is the chocolate mousse; easy to make, quick to set and, above all, rich and delicious. Other devotees are numerous, which is why there are no less than seven mousse recipes in this chapter, plus the Pots de Chocolat on page 109.

Iced desserts are also, of course, extremely popular. Although one can buy excellent commercially produced ice cream, there is nothing to beat home-made. I make no excuses for the fact that, with few exceptions, they are all fairly extravagant, being made with eggs and fresh cream. If you are going to go to the extra trouble of making it yourself, the result must be superb.

Do look also at the Large Cakes and Gâteaux in the book as well as the Classic recipes. Many of these make excellent desserts.

Crunchy Chocolate Mousse

This is a very economical chocolate mousse, not rich and, therefore, excellent for children.

15 g / ¹⁄₂ oz powdered gelatine
4 × 15 ml spoons / 4 tablespoons cold water
450 ml / ³⁄₄ pint milk
3 eggs, separated
25 g / 1 oz caster sugar
1 × 2.5 ml spoon / ¹⁄₂ teaspoon vanilla essence
100 g / 4 oz plain chocolate, broken into small pieces

TOPPING

25 g / 1 oz butter
50 g / 2 oz fresh brown breadcrumbs
25 g / 1 oz soft brown sugar

Sprinkle the gelatine over the water in a basin and leave to soften for 5 minutes. Pour the milk into a pan and bring up to blood temperature. Beat the egg yolks with the sugar and vanilla essence in a basin or the top of a double saucepan until thick and creamy. Pour in the milk. Put over a pan of gently simmering water and cook until the custard has thickened, stirring all the time. Stir in the softened gelatine and, when this has dissolved, add the chocolate, and stir until melted. Remove from the heat and put to one side until the mixture begins to thicken. Stir from time to time.

Whisk the egg whites until they form stiff peaks, then fold into the chocolate mixture. Turn into a shallow serving dish and chill in a refrigerator for at least 1 hour or until set.

To make the topping, melt the butter in a frying pan and fry the breadcrumbs until crisp and golden, stirring frequently. Remove from the heat and stir in the sugar. Sprinkle the crumbs over the mousse shortly before serving.

Serves 6–8

VARIATION   *Spread a layer of whipped cream between the mousse and the fried breadcrumbs.*

Chocolate and Crème de Menthe Mousses

275 g / 10 oz plain chocolate, broken into pieces

4 eggs, separated

3 × 15 ml spoons / 3 tablespoons crème de menthe

DECORATION

chocolate curls (page 12)

Place 12 paper cake cases in patty tins. Melt 175 g/ 6 oz of the chocolate (page 10). Divide between the paper cases and, with the back of a teaspoon, spread evenly over the base and sides of the cases. Put in a cool place for at least 30 minutes, or until the chocolate is quite hard.

Peel off the paper cases carefully. Melt the remaining chocolate (page 10) and remove from the heat. Beat in the egg yolks and the crème de menthe. Whisk the egg whites until they form stiff peaks, then fold into the chocolate mixture. Spoon into the prepared cases and chill in a refrigerator for at least 1 hour. Decorate each mousse with a chocolate curl before serving.

Makes 12

Bitter Chocolate and Orange Mousse

If you enjoy fresh orange juice, this mousse looks very attractive set in halved orange shells.

175 g / 6 oz plain chocolate, broken into pieces

grated rind and juice of 1 large orange

1 × 15 ml spoon / 1 tablespoon cocoa powder

2 × 15 ml spoons / 2 tablespoons Grand Marnier or Cointreau

3 eggs, separated

150 ml / ¼ pint double cream

DECORATION

whipped cream (optional)

grated orange rind or thin matchsticks of orange rind

Melt the chocolate (page 10) with the orange rind and juice and the cocoa. Remove from the heat and beat in the liqueur and egg yolks. Whip the cream until it holds its shape, and whisk the egg whites until stiff. Fold, first, the cream and then the egg whites into the chocolate mixture. Turn into six ramekin dishes and chill in a refrigerator for at least 1 hour. Decorate each mousse with a heaped teaspoonful of whipped cream, if liked, and a little orange rind before serving.

Serves 6

Almond Mousse

A chocolate mousse made very special by the burnt almonds.

175 g/6 oz plain chocolate **or** *cake covering, broken into pieces*

100 g/4 oz butter, preferably unsalted

100 g/4 oz caster sugar

2 eggs, separated

175 g/6 oz ground almonds

150 ml/¼ pint double cream

DECORATION

50 g/2 oz blanched whole almonds

150 ml/¼ pint double cream

Thoroughly clean and polish a 600 ml/1 pint jelly mould. Melt the chocolate (page 10), and use to coat the inside of the mould, as when making Easter eggs (page 15); you may find it easier to do this in two layers. When the chocolate is hard, remove from the mould, (do not worry if it cracks very slightly as you can hide this with piping when decorating).

Cream together the butter and sugar until light and fluffy, then beat in the egg yolks, one at a time. Fold in the ground almonds. Whip the cream lightly until it holds its shape. Whisk the egg whites until stiff. Fold, first, the cream and then the egg whites into the mixture. Turn into the chocolate mould and chill in a refrigerator for at least 2 hours.

Invert the mould on to a serving plate. Put the almonds on a piece of foil and toast under the grill until *very lightly* burnt. Remove and leave to cool. Whip the cream until stiff, and pile on the top and edges of the chocolate mould. Decorate with the burnt almonds.

Serves 6–8

Chocolate and Raspberry Layer Mousse

When I make this, I often set it in a glass dish and, while the raspberry mousse is setting, I tilt the dish on its side so that the mouse sets diagonally across the dish. I then pour the chocolate mousse on top and stand the dish upright to give a diagonal effect. Alternatively, it can be set in individual glasses.

RASPBERRY MOUSSE
350 g / 12 oz fresh raspberries

1½ × 5 ml spoons / 1½ teaspoons powdered gelatine

2 × 15 ml spoons / 2 tablespoons cold water

2 eggs, separated

50 g / 2 oz caster sugar

*150 ml / ¼ pint double **or** whipping cream*

CHOCOLATE MOUSSE
175 g / 6 oz plain chocolate, broken into pieces

2 × 5 ml spoons / 2 teaspoons instant coffee granules

1 × 15 ml spoon / 1 tablespoon water

4 eggs, separated

*150 ml / ¼ pint double **or** whipping cream*

DECORATION
150 ml / ¼ pint whipped cream (optional)

a few fresh raspberries

Rub the raspberries through a sieve, or purée in a blender or food processor. Sprinkle the gelatine over the cold water in a basin and leave to soften for 5 minutes. Stand over a pan of simmering water and leave until the gelatine has dissolved. Remove from the heat and allow to cool slightly. Whisk the egg yolks with the sugar until thick and creamy, then whisk in the gelatine. Stir in the raspberry purée and blend well. Whip the cream lightly until it holds its shape. Whisk the egg whites until stiff. Fold, first, the cream and then the egg whites into the raspberry mixture. Pour into a glass dish, and chill in a refrigerator for about 30 minutes.

Melt the chocolate with the coffee granules and water (page 10). Remove from the heat and beat in the egg yolks. Whip the cream lightly until it forms soft peaks. Whisk the egg whites until stiff. Fold, first, the cream and then the egg whites into the chocolate mixture. Pour over the chocolate mousse, and chill for at least 1 hour. Decorate with whipped cream, if liked, and raspberries before serving.

Serves 6–8

Strawberry Chocolate Box

With imported strawberries available throughout the year, this is a superb mousse to serve on special occasions. I have made it for Easter lunch when it seems particularly appropriate with its theme of chocolate.

225 g/8 oz plain chocolate, broken into pieces

15 g/½ oz vegetable shortening

FILLING

175 g/6 oz plain chocolate, broken into pieces

2 egg yolks

1 × 15 ml spoon/1 tablespoon Kirsch

150 ml/¼ pint double cream

150 ml/¼ pint single cream

TOPPING

225 g/8 oz fresh strawberries, hulled and halved **or** *quartered*

3 × 15 ml spoons/3 tablespoons strawberry jam, sieved

1 × 15 ml spoon/1 tablespoon Kirsch

25 g/1 oz plain chocolate, broken into small pieces

150 ml/¼ pint double cream

Use either a deep 15 cm/6 inch square cake tin or a 17.5 cm/7 inch square tin about 5 cm/2 inches deep. Line it with a large piece of double thickness foil cut in the corners. Ensure that there is enough foil above the top of the tin to pull the set chocolate out (see below).

Melt the chocolate with the vegetable shortening (page 10), pour two-thirds into the tin, then turn and tilt the tin to give an even coating over the sides and base. Allow to set, then repeat with the remaining chocolate and leave to set for about 30 minutes, or until it is quite hard. Remove from the tin by pulling the foil lining carefully. Peel the foil away from the chocolate case gently.

To make the filling, melt the chocolate (page 10), remove from the heat and beat in the egg yolks and Kirsch. Whip together the double and single creams until thick, then fold in the chocolate mixture. Pour into the prepared chocolate case and chill in a refrigerator until set.

Arrange the strawberries in the centre of the case, on top of the filling. Put the jam into a small pan, stir in the Kirsch and bring to the boil. Remove from the heat and allow to cool slightly. Spoon the topping over the strawberries; take care not to allow the hot jam to run to the edge of the chocolate case, or it will melt it. Leave for about 5 minutes for the glaze to set. Melt the chocolate (page 10) and allow to cool. Whip the double cream until stiff, then beat in the cooled chocolate. Spoon into a piping bag and pipe neatly round the edge of the case.

Chocolate Creams

The melted chocolate topping is a rather unusual way of presenting this rich custard recipe.

4 egg yolks
50 g / 2 oz caster sugar
1 × 2.5 ml spoon / ½ teaspoon vanilla essence
300 ml / ½ pint double cream
300 ml / ½ pint single cream
100 g / 4 oz plain chocolate cake covering, broken into pieces
2 × 15 ml spoons / 2 tablespoons vegetable oil

DECORATION
whipped cream

Butter six ramekin dishes. Beat the egg yolks lightly with the sugar and vanilla essence. Mix together the double and single creams and heat to blood temperature. Whisk into the egg yolks.

Turn the mixture into the prepared dishes, cover with foil and stand in a roasting tin containing 2.5 cm / 1 inch cold water. Bake in a warm oven, 160°C / 325°F / Gas 3, for about 30 minutes, or until set. Remove from the oven, take out of the water and leave to cool for about 1 hour.

Melt the chocolate with the oil (page 10); this makes it softer for serving. Spoon over the creams, then chill for at least 6 hours. Top each cream with a spoonful of whipped cream before serving.

Serves 6

Chocolate and Almond Layer Pudding

This Polish recipe is extremely rich and quite exquisite.

50 g / 2 oz plain chocolate, broken into pieces
50 g / 2 oz unsalted butter
75 g / 3 oz caster sugar
a few drops vanilla essence
50 g / 2 oz ground almonds
juice of ½ lemon

TOPPING
25 g / 1 oz plain chocolate, broken into pieces
25 g / 1 oz butter
150 ml / ¼ pint double cream

Melt the chocolate (page 10) and cool slightly. Cream the butter, beat in 25 g / 1 oz sugar and the vanilla essence. Beat until smooth and fluffy, then beat in the chocolate. Turn into a small glass serving dish and spread evenly. Chill for at least 30 minutes. Mix the almonds with the remaining sugar and lemon juice and spread evenly over the chocolate mixture. Chill while preparing the topping.

Melt the chocolate with the butter (page 10) and remove from the heat. Whip the cream lightly and fold gently into the chocolate. Spoon the topping over the chilled mixture, forming the cream into swirls. Chill in a refrigerator until ready to serve.

Serves 4–6

Apricot Fruit Basket

I made this chocolate basket using a foil container as a mould, approximately 22.5 × 12.5 cm/ 9 × 5 inches and 5 cm/2 inches deep. To fill the basket, any favourite fruit in season can be used as an alternative to apricots. Apricot, peach or rose leaves, washed and dried, make a pretty decoration if placed round the edge of the basket. If you do not wish to make the handle, use the extra chocolate to make the basket a little thicker.

200 g/7 oz milk chocolate **or** *milk chocolate cake covering, broken into pieces*

675 g/1½ lb fresh apricots, halved and stoned

25 g/1 oz sugar

4 × 15 ml spoons/4 tablespoons white wine

300 ml/½ pint double cream

Melt the chocolate (page 10), and use all but about 3 × 15 ml spoons/3 tablespoons to coat the inside of a foil container evenly (see above); use about a third of the melted chocolate at a time, so that it sets quickly. Leave to set in a cool place for at least 30 minutes.

To make the handle, spoon the remainder of the chocolate either into a greaseproof icing bag or into a nylon piping bag fitted with a small writing pipe; (keep the bowl used for melting the chocolate over the pan of hot water). Draw a circle, about 1.25 cm/ ½ inch smaller than the width of the foil dish, on a piece of waxed paper or non-stick silicone paper. Pipe a simple trellis pattern round this circle; the easiest one is one wavy line followed by a second wavy line in the opposite direction on top. Leave to set, then carefully cut into two semi-circles, using a sharp knife. Brush the smooth side of one of these with the chocolate remaining in the bowl (you only need a very little), then place the second semi-circle on top, again smooth side down. Leave to set.

Put half the apricots into a blender or food processor, and purée with the sugar and white wine. Whip the cream until it just holds its shape, then carefully fold in the apricot purée.

When the chocolate in the container is quite hard, loosen the foil very gently, and peel away from the chocolate. Spoon the apricot fool into the chocolate case. Arrange the remaining apricot halves on the top, piling them up to look like fruit in a basket. Place the handle in position, pressing it gently into the fool. Decorate with fruit leaves, if liked.

Serves 6–8

Avocado Fool

This is a recipe from the South Pacific.

2 large, ripe avocadoes, peeled and stoned
juice of 2 limes
2 × 15 ml spoons/2 tablespoons icing sugar
2 × 15 ml spoons/2 tablespoons brandy
150 ml/¼ pint double cream
75 g/3 oz milk chocolate, grated coarsely

Mash the avocadoes or purée in a blender or food processor with the lime juice and sugar, then add the brandy. Whip the cream until it holds its shape, then fold in the avocado purée. Taste, adding a little extra sugar if necessary, then turn into four individual bowls or glasses. Sprinkle the chocolate over the fools before serving.

Serves 4

Chocolate Chip Meringue Nests

I have suggested using frozen raspberries so that the dessert can be made at any time of year, but when fresh raspberries are in season, simply spread the bases of the meringue nests with whipped cream and top with the fresh fruit.

2 egg whites
100 g/4 oz caster sugar
50 g/2 oz plain chocolate cake covering, grated

FILLING

350 g/12 oz frozen raspberries, thawed
1 × 15 ml spoon/1 tablespoon cornflour
1 × 15 ml spoon/1 tablespoon sugar
4 × 15 ml spoons/4 tablespoons whipped cream

Draw four circles, each 10 cm/4 inches in diameter, on a piece of non-stick silicone paper. Oil both sides lightly and place on a baking sheet. Whisk the egg whites until they form stiff peaks, then whisk in half the sugar, 1 × 5 ml spoon/1 teaspoon at a time until the mixture is stiff and shiny. Fold in the remaining sugar with the chocolate. Divide the meringue mixture between the four circles, building up the sides, so that a 'nest' is formed. Bake in a very cool oven, 120°C/250°F/Gas ½, for about 2 hours or until quite dry. Remove from the oven, leave to cool, then peel off the paper carefully. Place on a dish.

To make the filling, drain the raspberries and blend the juice with the cornflour in a small pan. Add the sugar and bring to the boil, stirring all the time, until thickened. Stir in the raspberries, remove from the heat and leave to cool.

Up to 1 hour before serving, fill the nests with the raspberry mixture and top each one with a spoonful of whipped cream. Chill until ready to serve.

Serves 4

Hazelnut and Orange Torte

2 eggs, separated

175 g / 6 oz caster sugar

75 g / 3 oz plain chocolate, broken into pieces

100 g / 4 oz butter

50 g / 2 oz hazelnuts, chopped

2 × 15 ml spoons / 2 tablespoons Cointreau

150 ml / ¼ pint orange juice

24 sponge finger biscuits

150 ml / ¼ pint double cream

Oil a baking sheet lightly and line with non-stick silicone paper. Whisk the egg whites until stiff, then whisk in 100 g / 4 oz of the sugar, 1 × 5 ml spoon / 1 teaspoon at a time, until the mixture is stiff and shiny. Put in a piping bag fitted with a large rose nozzle, and pipe small meringues, about 3.5 cm / 1½ inches in diameter, to make about 20. Bake in a very cool oven, 120°C / 250°F / Gas ½, for about 2 hours or until the meringues are crisp. Remove from the oven and leave to cool.

Butter a 900 g / 2 lb loaf tin lightly and line with non-stick silicone paper. Melt the chocolate (page 10), remove from the heat and cool slightly. Cream together the butter and remaining sugar until light and fluffy, then beat in the chocolate and hazelnuts. Mix the Cointreau with the orange juice. Dip each sponge finger into the orange mixture for a few seconds, then arrange one-third of them on the base of the tin, sugar side outwards. Spread with half the chocolate mixture. Repeat for the next layer, and finish with a layer of sponge fingers. Cover with a piece of foil, and place a weight on top. Chill in a refrigerator for at least 2 hours, then remove from the tin. Whip the cream until stiff and spread over the cake. Decorate with the meringues.

Serves 6–8

The Chocolate Mousse
Chocolate and Raspberry Layer Mousse (page 69), Chocolate and Crème de Menthe Mousses (page 67), Bitter Chocolate and Orange Mousse (page 67) **and** *Almond Mousse (page 68)*

OVERLEAF LEFT   Chocolate and Strawberry Bombe (page 85)
OVERLEAF RIGHT   Marbled Ice (page 83), Mocha Ice Cream (page 82) **and** *Chocolate Chip Brown Bread Ice Cream (page 83)*

Tia Maria Soufflé

Cold soufflés are very elegant and not difficult to make.

15 g/½ oz powdered gelatine

4 × 15 ml spoons/4 tablespoons cold water

450 ml/¾ pint milk

3 eggs, separated

50 g/2 oz caster sugar

1 × 5 ml spoon/1 teaspoon vanilla essence

15 g/½ oz plain flour, sifted

225 g/8 oz plain chocolate, broken into small pieces

4 × 15 ml spoons/4 tablespoons Tia Maria

300 ml/½ pint whipping cream

DECORATION

whipped cream

chocolate leaves **or** horns (page 13)

Make a collar for a 900 ml/1½ pint soufflé dish, using a piece of double greaseproof or non-stick silicone paper; the collar should stand at least 10 cm/4 inches above the rim of the soufflé dish. Brush one side of the piece of paper with oil or butter, wrap round the soufflé dish, the greased side facing inwards, and tie in position with string.

Sprinkle the gelatine over the water in a basin and leave to soften for 5 minutes. Pour the milk into a pan and bring to the boil. Whisk the egg yolks lightly with the sugar and vanilla essence, then beat in the flour. Pour over the boiling milk, stirring well. Return the mixture to the pan and bring to the boil, stirring all the time, then cook for 2–3 minutes. Remove from the heat and stir in the softened gelatine; leave until dissolved. Add the chocolate and stir until melted. Stir in the Tia Maria. Cover with clingfilm and leave to cool.

Whip the cream until it forms soft peaks, then whisk the egg whites until stiff. Fold, first, the cream and then the egg whites into the chocolate custard. Turn the mixture into the prepared dish. Chill in a refrigerator for at least 2 hours.

Before serving, peel off the paper collar carefully, easing it off with a knife. Decorate the top of the soufflé with piped cream and chocolate leaves or horns.

Serves 6

A Selection of Drinks
Coffee Choco (page 91), Crunchy Peppermint Milk Shake (page 93), Iced Chocolate (page 93) **and** *Caribbean Chocolate (page 92)*

Marbled Savarin

This is an ideal dessert for a buffet party and one that can be made all the year round. Use whatever fruit is in season, such as pears, cherries, peaches and strawberries; choose only ripe perfect fruit, and peel, stone and slice as necessary. If catering for smaller numbers, use half quantities and bake in a 17.5 cm/7 inch ring tin.

115 g/4½oz butter
250 ml/8 fl oz milk
1 × 5 ml spoon/1 teaspoon sugar
2½ × 5 ml spoons/2½ teaspoons dried yeast
300 g/11 oz plain flour
a pinch of salt
3 eggs, beaten
25 g/1 oz cocoa powder

SYRUP AND FILLING

675 g/1½lb sugar
600 ml/1 pint water
150 ml/¼ pint dark rum
900 g/2 lb prepared fresh fruit (see above)

Grease and flour a 22.5 cm/9 inch ring tin. Melt the butter in a pan, then leave to cool. Heat the milk to blood temperature, then pour into a basin. Stir in the sugar and sprinkle with the yeast. Leave in a warm place for 10 minutes or until frothy. Sift together 275 g/10 oz of the flour with the salt into a mixing bowl. Make a hollow in the centre, pour in the yeast mixture and the eggs, and mix well with a wooden spoon to make a smooth dough. Beat in the cooled butter, and beat for a further 2–3 minutes. Divide the mixture in half. Sift the remaining flour into one half and the cocoa into the other half. Beat both batters until smooth.

Put alternate spoonfuls of the mixtures into the prepared tin. Cover with a piece of oiled clingfilm and put into a warm place for about 40 minutes, or until the dough has risen almost to the top of the tin. Bake in a hot oven, 220°C/425°F/Gas 7, for about 25 minutes, or until golden-brown and firm. Cool in the tin for 5 minutes, then turn out on to a wire rack with a plate underneath.

Make the syrup while the savarin is cooking. Put the sugar into a pan with the water and stir over low heat until the sugar has dissolved. Bring to the boil, then remove from the heat and stir in the rum.

While the savarin is still hot, prick it all over with a fine skewer and pour over the warm rum syrup, a little at a time. When all the syrup has been used, pour any which has drained on to the plate back into the pan. Pour over the savarin again. Repeat until only about 150 ml/¼ pint is left. Carefully place the savarin on a serving dish. Mix the remaining syrup with the fruit, and spoon this into the centre of the savarin. Serve with whipped cream.

Serves 12

Crackolate Cheesecake

The base of this cheesecake is the ever-popular crackolate mixture, which is normally made in small paper cake cases. Made with rice krispies as here, rather than with cornflakes, it makes an unusual and delicious base for an uncooked cheesecake.

50g/2oz butter

2 × 15 ml spoons/2 tablespoons golden syrup

2 × 15 ml spoons/2 tablespoons
granulated sugar

2 × 15 ml spoons/2 tablespoons
cocoa powder

65g/2½oz rice krispies

FILLING

350g/12oz strawberries, hulled

350g/12oz cottage cheese

15g/½oz powdered gelatine

4 × 15 ml spoons/4 tablespoons cold water

2 eggs, separated

75g/3oz caster sugar

grated rind of 1 lemon

150ml/¼ pint whipping cream

DECORATION

150ml/¼ pint whipping cream

chocolate leaves (page 13)

Lightly oil a loose-bottomed 20cm/8 inch cake tin. Put the butter, syrup, sugar and cocoa into a pan and stir over low heat until the butter has melted and the sugar dissolved. Remove from the heat and stir in the rice krispies. Spread evenly over the bottom of the prepared tin and leave to set for 30 minutes.

To make the filling, rub the strawberries with the cottage cheese through a sieve, or purée in a blender or food processor. Sprinkle the gelatine over the cold water in a basin and leave to soften for 5 minutes. Stand over a pan of simmering water and leave until the gelatine has dissolved. Remove from the heat and allow to cool slightly. Whisk the egg yolks with the sugar and lemon rind until thick and creamy. Whisk the egg whites until stiff. Whip the cream until stiff. Stir the strawberry and cheese purée into the egg yolk mixture, stir in the gelatine, then fold in the cream and finally the egg whites. Turn into the prepared tin on top of the chocolate base and leave to set for at least 2 hours.

To serve, carefully push the cake out of the tin from the base. Loosen the base with a palette knife and transfer to a serving dish, using a fish slice. Whip the cream, and spread evenly over the top of the cake. Decorate with the chocolate leaves.

Serves 6–8

Chocolate and Ginger Cheesecake

200 g/7 oz ginger biscuits

75 g/3 oz butter

1 × 15 ml spoon/1 tablespoon
Demerara sugar

FILLING

100 g/4 oz plain chocolate, broken
into pieces

225 g/8 oz cream cheese

2 × 15 ml spoons/2 tablespoons ginger syrup

3 × 15 ml spoons/3 tablespoons single cream

2 eggs, separated

3 pieces preserved stem ginger,
chopped finely

DECORATION

4 × 15 ml spoons/4 tablespoons whipped
cream (approx)

1–2 pieces preserved stem ginger, sliced

Crush the biscuits with a rolling-pin between the folds of a tea-towel, or use a food processor. Melt the butter in a small pan, remove from the heat and stir in the biscuits and sugar. Press into a 20–22.5 cm/8–9 inch flan ring, tin or dish, and chill.

To make the filling, melt the chocolate (page 10). Remove from the heat. Beat the cream cheese with the ginger syrup and single cream, then beat in the egg yolks, one at a time, followed by the chocolate and ginger. Whisk the egg whites until stiff, then fold into the cream cheese mixture.

Turn the mixture into the biscuit cases and chill in a refrigerator for at least 1 hour. Decorate with whipped cream, piped or swirled on the top, and small pieces of stem ginger.

Serves 6

Mocha Ice Cream

100 g/4 oz soft brown sugar

4 × 15 ml spoons/4 tablespoons
cocoa powder

2 × 15 ml spoons/2 tablespoons instant
coffee granules

50 g/2 oz butter

5 × 15 ml spoons/5 tablespoons water

400 g/14 oz canned evaporated milk

Put the sugar, cocoa, coffee, butter and water into a pan. Heat gently, stirring until melted, then bring to the boil. Leave to cool. Pour the evaporated milk into a large mixing bowl. Whisk until thick and frothy and the whisk leaves a trail, then whisk in the cooled sauce until well blended.

Turn the mixture into a freezer and leave until partially frozen. Remove and beat well. Pour into a freezer container, freeze until firm, then cover.

Serves 6

Note *Evaporated milk can be whipped if it is at room temperature, but it whips better if chilled overnight.*

Chocolate Chip Brown Bread Ice Cream

Most recipes for brown bread ice cream suggest toasting the breadcrumbs before use, so that they give a crisp texture. This is not quite as easy as it sounds, as the crumbs easily burn unless turned frequently. Adding chocolate to the mixture not only enhances the flavour, but also gives a crunchy texture without any of the bother.

300 ml / ½ pint double cream
150 ml / ¼ pint single cream
2 eggs, separated
75 g / 3 oz icing sugar, sifted
100 g / 4 oz wholemeal breadcrumbs
50 g / 2 oz plain chocolate, grated coarsely **or** chopped finely

Lightly whip the double and single creams together until they hold their shape. Whisk the egg yolks and icing sugar until thick and creamy, then stir in the breadcrumbs and chocolate. Fold into the whipped cream. Whisk the egg whites until they form stiff peaks, then fold into the cream. Turn the mixture into a 1.2 litre/2 pint freezer container and freeze for 2–3 hours until firm.

Serves 6

Marbled Ice

300 ml / ½ pint milk
75 g / 3 oz caster sugar
4 egg yolks
300 ml / ½ pint double cream
1 × 2.5 ml spoon / ½ teaspoon vanilla essence
75 g / 3 oz plain chocolate, broken into pieces

Heat the milk with the sugar to blood temperature. Whisk the egg yolks, then pour over the hot milk, whisking all the time. Return the mixture to the pan and stir over very low heat until the custard thickens; take great care not to curdle the mixture. Remove from the heat, cover the pan with clingfilm and leave to cool.

Whip the cream very lightly; it should be just slightly thickened. Whisk the cooled custard and fold into the cream. Pour half the mixture into a plastic container and stir in the vanilla essence.

Melt the chocolate (page 10), and stir into the remaining mixture. Carefully pour the chocolate mixture in a zigzag pattern over the vanilla ice. Stir very lightly with a spoon to give a marbled appearance. Freeze for at least 4 hours.

Serves 6–8

Chocolate Tutti Frutti Bombe

This makes a spectacular dessert for a dinner party, especially when served at the table flaming. Any left over can be stored in a freezer.

225 g/8 oz plain chocolate cake covering, broken into pieces

3 eggs, separated

75 g/3 oz icing sugar, sifted

300 ml/½ pint double cream

100 g/4 oz glacé cherries, chopped

100 g/4 oz dried apricots, chopped

100 g/4 oz candied peel, chopped

100 g/4 oz blanched almonds, chopped

5 × 15 ml spoons/5 tablespoons brandy **or** dark rum

Put a 1.8 litre/3 pint pudding basin (a plastic one is ideal) in the freezer for a few minutes. Melt the chocolate (page 10). Remove the basin and pour in the chocolate. Roll it round and round until the inside is coated evenly. Leave to set.

Whisk the egg yolks with 25 g/1 oz of the sugar until thick and creamy. Whisk the egg whites until stiff, then whisk in the remaining sugar, 1 × 5 ml/1 teaspoon at a time. Whisk in the egg yolks gradually. Whip the cream lightly. Fold all the fruit and nuts into the egg mixture, then fold in the cream. Turn the mixture into the prepared basin. If the ice cream level does not quite reach the level of the chocolate, neaten off with a sharp knife. Any excess chocolate can be chopped and stirred into the ice cream mixture. Cover the basin and freeze for at least 4 hours or until quite firm.

To turn the pudding out, dip into a bowl of very hot water for about 1 minute and invert on to a plate; replace in the freezer. About 30 minutes before serving, place on a serving plate and put in the refrigerator; (do not use the plate that has been in the freezer as this will prevent the alcohol from igniting.)

Put the brandy or rum into a small pan and heat gently, then pour over the pudding, and ignite.

Serves 8–12

Note   *It does not matter if the chocolate covering is not smoothly coated, as it will not be visible once the bombe is filled with ice cream.*

Chocolate and Strawberry Bombe

CHOCOLATE ICE CREAM
4 egg yolks

75 g/3 oz caster sugar

600 ml/1 pint single cream

75 g/3 oz plain chocolate, broken into small pieces

STRAWBERRY ICE CREAM
350 g/12 oz fresh **or** frozen strawberries, thawed

4 egg yolks

75 g/3 oz caster sugar

450 ml/3/4 pint single cream

DECORATION (optional)
whipped cream

fresh strawberries **or** chocolate curls (page 12) **or** leaves (page 13)

Whisk the egg yolks and sugar in a basin over a pan of simmering water until thick and creamy. Heat the cream in a small pan to blood temperature. Stir into the egg yolks and cook over low heat, stirring all the time, until the mixture thickens. Remove from the heat and stir in the chocolate until melted. Pour into a 1.5 litre/2½ pint basin and leave to cool for about 1 hour. Put a 900 ml/1½ pint basin in the centre and place enough weights inside to bring the mixture level with the top of the basin. Freeze for at least 2 hours or until firm.

Pour a little hot water into the inner basin, and as soon as the ice cream round the edge starts to melt, remove it carefully. Return the ice cream to the freezer.

To make the strawberry ice cream, rub the strawberries through a sieve or purée in a blender or food processor. Using the egg yolks, sugar and cream, make the ice cream mixture as for the chocolate ice cream . Remove from the heat and stir in the strawberry purée. Cool for about 1 hour. Pour the strawberry ice cream into the cavity left in the centre of the chocolate ice cream, and freeze for a further 2–3 hours until quite firm.

To turn out, quickly dip the basin into a bowl of very hot water for a few seconds and invert on to a serving plate. Either serve the bombe as it is, or decorate with whipped cream and fresh strawberries, or chocolate curls or leaves.

Serves 8

Lemon Sorbet with Raspberry Sauce

If you use bought lemon sorbet, as I suggest, you can present an immaculate dessert with very little difficulty. Home-made sorbet can also, of course, be used.

500 ml/17 fl oz carton lemon sorbet
175 g/6 oz plain chocolate, broken into pieces
2 × 15 ml spoons/2 tablespoons vegetable oil
350 g/12 oz frozen raspberries, thawed
25 g/1 oz icing sugar

Using either a small ice-cream scoop, or a dessert-spoon, form the sorbet into 18 balls. Place on a piece of non-stick silicone or waxed paper on a tray and put into a freezer for about 10 minutes to harden.

Melt the chocolate with the oil (page 10) and allow to cool slightly. Spoon a little chocolate carefully over each ball of sorbet, coating them evenly. Return the tray to the freezer for at least 15 minutes.

Reserve six raspberries for decoration. Rub the remaining raspberries through a sieve or purée in a blender or food processor (then sieve the purée to remove the seeds). Stir in the icing sugar. To serve, divide the sauce between six plates, top with three balls of chocolate-covered sorbet and decorate each one with a raspberry.

Serves 6

VARIATION   *Different flavours of sorbet, and combinations of flavours, can be used.*

Layered Log Ice Cream

A marvellous way of turning a block of commercially made ice cream into an elegant dinner party dessert with the minimum of time, effort and money.

2 × 5 ml spoons/2 teaspoons instant coffee granules
1 × 15 ml spoon/1 tablespoon Tia Maria **or** rum
50 g/2 oz hazelnuts
50 g/2 oz desiccated coconut
1 rounded 15 ml spoon/1 rounded tablespoon chocolate spread
1 × 15 ml spoon/1 tablespoon milk **or** coconut liqueur
2 litres/3½ pints vanilla ice cream
75 g/3 oz plain chocolate, broken into pieces

Dissolve the coffee in the Tia Maria or rum. Toast the hazelnuts under a moderate grill for a few minutes. Remove from the heat and, when cool enough to handle, rub them together until the skins come off. Replace the nuts under the grill and cook until golden-brown, taking care that they do not burn, then chop them very finely by hand or with a blender or food processor.

Lightly toast the coconut, making sure it all becomes evenly golden and does not burn. Blend the chocolate spread with the milk or coconut liqueur to form a smooth paste.

Divide the ice cream into three portions; leave two in the freezer and place the third in a mixing bowl. Chop this roughly into about six portions and leave to soften for about 5 minutes. Pour in the coffee mixture, then beat well (preferably with an electric beater). Turn into a 900 g/2 lb loaf tin, spread evenly over the base, then replace in the freezer for about 10 minutes until quite firm.

Remove a second portion of ice cream, chop and soften as before and beat in the hazelnuts. Spread this over the coffee ice cream and leave to harden in the freezer.

Finally, beat the chocolate spread and coconut liquer into the last portion of ice cream, spread over the hazelnut mixture and chill for at least 1 hour.

To turn the ice cream out, quickly dip the tin into a bowl of very hot water for a few seconds, and invert on to a plate. Replace in the freezer for 5 minutes. Melt the chocolate and drizzle all over the top and sides of the ice cream (page 13). Replace in the freezer until ready to serve.

Serves 8

Chocolate Terrine with Cherry Sauce

This is a wonderful rich chocolate dessert. I have deliberately made a fairly large quantity as it is a marvellous standby for the freezer and you can just cut off a slice or two when you want it, Beware, however, it is very rich so you will not want much!

225 g/8 oz plain chocolate, broken into pieces

225 g/8 oz unsalted butter

50 g/2 oz icing sugar

50 g/2 oz cocoa powder

4 egg yolks

100 g/4 oz granulated sugar

150 ml/¼ pint water

300 ml/½ pint double cream

100 g/4 oz pitted black cherries (fresh **or** frozen), chopped roughly

SAUCE

450 g/1 lb pitted black cherries (fresh **or** frozen)

300 ml/10 fl oz water

100 g/4 oz sugar

2 × 15 ml spoons/2 tablespoons cornflour

4 × 15 ml spoons/4 tablespoons Kirsch (optional)

Butter a 1.2 kg/3 lb loaf tin. Melt the chocolate (page 10). Remove from the heat and leave to cool slightly. Cream the butter until light and fluffy. Sift the icing sugar and cocoa together and beat into the butter alternately with the chocolate. Beat the egg yolks lightly in a separate basin. Put the sugar and water into a small, heavy-based pan and stir over low heat until the sugar has dissolved. Boil rapidly to 103°C/225°F on a sugar thermometer (thread stage). Beat into the egg yolks, a little at a time, and whisk to a mousse-like consistency. Beat slowly into the butter mixture. Whip the cream lightly, then fold into the chocolate mixture. Fold in the cherries last. Turn into the prepared tin and freeze for at least 6 hours or until firm. Serve each portion with about 2 × 15 ml spoons/2 tablespoons of hot cherry sauce.

To make the cherry sauce, put the cherries, all but 3 × 15 ml spoons/3 tablespoons of the water and the sugar into a pan, and bring to the boil. Blend the cornflour with the remaining water, stir into the pan and bring back to the boil, stirring all the time. Remove from the heat and stir in the Kirsch, if used.

Terrine serves 12–16
Sauce serves 8–10

VARIATION   *Serve the Terrine with warm Chocolate Fudge Sauce (page 91) instead of the Cherry Sauce.*

Sauces and Drinks

Chocolate sauce is the perfect accompaniment for ice cream and numerous other desserts, both hot and cold. Use any of the recipes in this chapter and see how easy it is to transform a simple dessert into something quite special.

If you want to make a chocolate sauce which is not too sweet, use bitter chocolate as this produces a really excellent rich sauce. Try any of these recipes using bitter chocolate, and add just a very little extra sugar.

Chocolate milk shakes are always popular and for these you can use either a commercial syrup or drinking chocolate. The home-made syrup on page 93 is, however, extremely useful as it keeps in a refrigerator for weeks.

Rich Chocolate Sauce (1)

Since this sauce can be served at any temperature, it is ideal for most desserts, but especially profiteroles and ice cream. If you are serving it cold, add about 3 × 15 ml spoons/3 tablespoons single cream to keep it at a pouring consistency.

1 rounded 15 ml spoon/1 rounded tablespoon cocoa powder

175 g/6 oz canned evaporated milk

75 g/3 oz plain chocolate, broken into small pieces

Whisk together the cocoa and evaporated milk in a small pan. Put over low heat and bring to boiling point. Remove from the heat and stir in the chocolate. Return to low heat and continue stirring until the chocolate has melted.

Serves 4–6

Rich Chocolate Sauce (2)

A richer sauce than the previous recipe.

100 g / 4 oz butter
100 g / 4 oz caster sugar
a pinch of salt
2 × 15 ml spoons / 2 tablespoons dark rum
50 g / 2 oz cocoa powder
150 ml / ¼ pint double cream
1 × 5 ml spoon / 1 teaspoon vanilla essence

Melt the butter in a small pan. Stir in the sugar, salt, rum and the cocoa. Mix well over low heat. Add the cream and bring to the boil. Simmer very gently for 5 minutes. Remove from the heat and add the vanilla essence. Serve hot or cold.

Serves 6–8

Chocolate and Orange Sauce

150 ml / ¼ pint fresh orange juice
grated rind of 1 orange
25 g / 1 oz butter
100 g / 4 oz milk chocolate drops

Heat the orange juice and rind, and the butter in a small pan and, when the butter has melted, bring to boiling point. Remove from the heat, stir in the chocolate and return to the heat, stirring all the time. When the chocolate has melted, boil for about 1 minute.

Serves 4–6

Note   *Orange juice from a carton can be used instead of the fresh orange juice and rind , but this does not give such a strong orange flavour to the sauce.*

Charlotte's Peppermint Sauce

A very sweet sauce, deemed 'delicious' by my eleven-year old niece. Perfect for ice cream.

75 g / 3 oz chocolate-covered peppermint creams
150 ml / ¼ pint single cream

Break each chocolate in half and melt in a basin over a pan of hot water. Remove from the heat and gradually stir in the cream. Serve warm or cold.

Serves 4–6

Chocolate Fudge Sauce

The sugar may be left out of this sauce if you prefer it less sweet, but its omission will tend to make the butter separate out. To rectify this, let the sauce cool a little, or leave until cold, and whisk just before serving. If you plan to serve it cold, add about 3 × 15 ml spoons/3 tablespoons single cream to keep it at a pouring consistency.

50 g/2 oz unsalted butter

120 ml/scant ¼ pint milk

25 g/1 oz caster sugar

100 g/4 oz plain chocolate, broken into small pieces

Put the butter, milk and sugar into a small pan and bring to the boil. Remove from the heat and add the chocolate. Stir until the chocolate has melted, then return to the heat and boil rapidly for 2 minutes.

Serves 4–6

Bitter Fudge Sauce

75 g/3 oz butter

50 g/2 oz bitter chocolate

50 g/2 oz granulated sugar

150 ml/¼ pint single cream

Put all the ingredients into a small pan. Put over a gentle heat, stirring frequently until the butter and chocolate have melted. Bring to the boil for about 1 minute, stirring all the time, until a smooth, thick sauce is obtained. Serve hot.

Serves 4–6

VARIATION *Flavour the sauce with rum, brandy or any liqueur. Add after the sauce has boiled.*

Coffee Choco

450 ml/¾ pint milk

450 ml/¾ pint water

1½ × 15 ml spoons/1½ tablespoons instant coffee granules

1 × 15 ml spoon/1 tablespoon drinking chocolate

4 chocolate flake bars

Heat the milk and water to just below boiling point. Blend in the coffee and chocolate, and mix well. Pour into glasses and put a chocolate flake into each glass.

Serves 4

Rum Toddy

An ideal warmer for a cold winter's day.

15 g / 1/2 oz plain chocolate, broken into pieces
150 ml / 1/4 pint milk
1 × 15 ml spoon / 1 tablespoon dark rum
1 heaped 5 ml spoon / 1 heaped teaspoon whipped cream
a little grated nutmeg

Put the chocolate and milk into a small pan and bring to the boil, stirring once or twice. Remove from the heat and whisk in the rum. Pour into a small cup or glass. Top with the cream and sprinkle with the nutmeg.

Serves 1

Caribbean Chocolate

250 ml / 8 fl oz milk
1 1/2 × 15 ml spoons / 1 1/2 tablespoons drinking chocolate
a good pinch of ground nutmeg
a good pinch of ground allspice
a good pinch of ground cinnamon
1 × 15 ml spoon / 1 tablespoon whipped cream
drinking chocolate

Put the milk, chocolate and spices into a pan and bring to the boil. Remove from the heat, whisk well and pour into a mug. Top with the whipped cream and sprinkle with a little extra drinking chocolate.

Serves 1

Quickie Milk Shake

3 rounded 15 ml spoons / 3 rounded tablespoons vanilla ice cream
2 × 15 ml spoons / 2 tablespoons drinking chocolate
150 ml / 1/4 pint milk

Blend all the ingredients in a blender or food processor for about 30 seconds. Serve immediately.

Serves 1

Crunchy Peppermint Milk Shake

The American hamburger chains have turned every child into a milk shake connoisseur. This one should prove very popular.

25 g / 1 oz plain chocolate cake covering
3 × 15 ml spoons / 3 tablespoons chocolate ice cream
150 ml / ¼ pint cold milk
½ × 2.5 ml spoon / ¼ teaspoon peppermint essence

Put the cake covering into a blender or food processor and chop finely. Add all the remaining ingredients and blend for a further 30 seconds until well mixed and frothy. Serve at once.

Serves 1

Iced Chocolate

Perfect for a hot summer's day.

300 ml / ½ pint milk
150 ml / ¼ pint single cream
3 × 15 ml spoons / 3 tablespoons Chocolate Syrup
8 ice cubes (approx)

Whisk together the milk, cream and syrup. Put the ice cubes into a jug, pour over the chocolate, and serve.

Serves 4

VARIATION *Top with small scoops of ice cream.*

Chocolate Syrup

This syrup is particularly useful as it can be kept in a covered container in a refrigerator for weeks. Use as a base for milk shakes, or pour over ice cream as a sauce and thin with a little milk.

275 g / 10 oz soft brown sugar
100 g / 4 oz cocoa powder
½ × 2.5 ml spoon / ¼ teaspoon salt
300 ml / ½ pint water
2 × 5 ml spoons / 2 teaspoons vanilla essence

Put all the ingredients, except the vanilla essence, into a pan, mix well and bring to the boil. Cook gently for 5 minutes, stirring frequently. Remove from the heat, leave to cool, then stir in the vanilla essence. Cover and chill in a refrigerator until required.

The Chocolate Classics

Most Western countries boast a 'classic' chocolate dish, many of which are closely identified with the food of that country. Think of Sacher Torte and you think of Austria, Schwarzwälderkirschtorte signifies Germany, Devil's Food Cake means the United States. These dishes are not just among the best chocolate recipes in the world, but some of the best of all recipes in the world, and I can certainly find a number of my all-time favourites among them. The following is just such a selection and to my mind, epitomizes what chocolate cookery is all about.

Classic Cakes
*Schwarzwälderkirschtorte (page 102),
Sacher Torte (page 104)* **and** *Dobos Torte
(page 101)*

Mole de Guajolote

The exact translation of Mole de Guajolote is Turkey with Mole Sauce which is a very well known Mexican dish served on feast days and holidays. An authentic mole sauce is, however, extremely complicated to make, requiring about three different kinds of chillies as well as special green tomatoes and other ingredients. I have, therefore, simplified the recipe considerably, using ingredients which are readily available, but have not detracted from a delicious authentic end result.

1 × 1.2 kg / 3 lb chicken
salt
1 × 5 ml spoon / 1 teaspoon black peppercorns
2 onions
2 × 15 ml spoons / 2 tablespoons oil
2 green chillies, deseeded and finely chopped
1 clove of garlic, crushed
4 cloves
½ × 2.5 ml spoon / ¼ teaspoon whole cumin seeds
1 × 2.5 ml spoon / ½ teaspoon ground cinnamon
2 × 15 ml spoons / 2 tablespoons ground almonds
2 × 15 ml spoons / 2 tablespoons sesame seeds
50 g / 2 oz cornmeal
400 g / 14 oz canned tomatoes
25 g / 1 oz plain chocolate, broken into pieces

Skin the chicken, bone it and cut the flesh into 2.5 cm / 1 inch cubes. Put the chicken skin and bones into a saucepan, with 1 × 5 ml spoon / 1 teaspoon salt, the peppercorns and 1 onion, roughly chopped. Cover with cold water and bring to the boil, then simmer gently for 45 minutes–1 hour.

Heat the oil in a large pan and gently fry the second onion, finely chopped, the chillies and garlic for 8 minutes. Remove from the heat and add all the remaining ingredients. Pour in 300 ml / ½ pint of the chicken stock. Return to the heat, bring to the boil, stirring all the time, then cover and cook over very low heat for 20 minutes, stirring frequently to prevent the ingredients from sticking to the pan. Rub through a sieve, or purée in a blender or food processor, then return to the pan.

Strain the remaining stock and gently poach the chicken pieces in it for about 10 minutes, then remove with a perforated spoon. Re-heat the mole sauce, add the chicken pieces and simmer for about 5 minutes. Season to taste.

Serve with boiled rice and tortillas, if available.

Serves 4

Saint Emilion au Chocolat (page 109)

Lepre con Agrodolce

Agrodolce is a classic Italian sauce, the origins of which can be traced back to the Romans. It is almost always served with game, such as hare, wild boar, wild duck and venison. The Spanish, who are great game eaters, also cook both hare and partridge in a chocolate sauce.

1 hare, skinned and jointed
300 ml / ½ pint red wine vinegar
300 ml / ½ pint water
50 g / 2 oz flour
salt and freshly ground black pepper
25 g / 1 oz butter
2 × 15 ml spoons / 2 tablespoons oil
100 g / 4 oz smoked bacon, chopped
300 ml / ½ pint red wine
300 ml / ½ pint stock
a sprig of thyme

SAUCE

50 g / 2 oz sugar
100 ml / 4 fl oz red wine vinegar
1 clove of garlic, crushed
25 g / 1 oz bitter chocolate
1 × 15 ml spoon / 1 tablespoon raisins

Put the hare joints in a dish. Mix together the wine and water, pour over the hare and leave to marinate for 4 hours, turning from time to time.

Remove the hare from the marinade and dry thoroughly. Coat with the flour seasoned with salt and pepper. Heat the butter and oil in a pan. Add the bacon and fry gently for 5 minutes. Remove and put to one side. Fry the pieces of hare, a few at a time, until brown. Put all the hare and the bacon back in the pan. Pour over the wine and stock, add the thyme, cover and cook gently for 1½ hours.

To make the sauce, put the sugar and vinegar into a small, heavy-based pan. Stir over low heat until the sugar has dissolved. Bring to the boil and boil rapidly to 176°C/345°F on a sugar thermometer (caramel stage). Remove from the heat and stir in the garlic and the chocolate. When the chocolate has melted, strain in 450 ml/¾ pint of the liquor from cooking the hare. Replace over gentle heat and simmer for about 5 minutes. Place the joints of hare on a serving dish and pour over the chocolate sauce.

Serves 6

American Brownies

There must be more different recipes for Brownies than there are states in America, but the one essential for a good Brownie is that it must have a soft and chewy centre.

75 g / 3 oz butter
50 g / 2 oz plain chocolate
175 g / 6 oz soft brown sugar
75 g / 3 oz self-raising flour, sifted
2 eggs, beaten
50 g / 2 oz walnuts, chopped roughly

Grease and flour a shallow 20 cm / 8 inch square cake tin. Melt the chocolate and butter (page 10). Remove from the heat and stir in the sugar. Beat in the flour and eggs until smooth. Stir in the walnuts.

Pour the mixture into the prepared tin and bake in a moderate oven, 180°C/350°F/Gas 4, for 35–40 minutes until well risen and firm to the touch; the inside should be slightly soft and the surface cracked. Cool slightly before cutting into squares or fingers.

Makes 16

Florentines

Florentines, often so inviting in the pâtisserie, are sometimes slightly disappointing when eaten because inferior chocolate has been used for coating them. A good quality chocolate makes all the difference.

50 g / 2 oz butter
50 g / 2 oz caster sugar
25 g / 1 oz plain flour, sifted
50 g / 2 oz blanched almonds, chopped
25 g / 1 oz glacé cherries, chopped
25 g / 1 oz candied peel, chopped
100 g / 4 oz plain chocolate, broken into pieces

Line two baking trays with non-stick silicone paper. Put the butter and sugar into a small pan and heat gently until melted. Remove from the heat and stir in the flour with the almonds, cherries and peel.

Drop spoonfuls of the mixture, well apart, on to the prepared baking trays. Bake in a moderate oven, 180°C/350°F/Gas 4, for about 10 minutes until golden-brown. Leave to cool on the baking sheets until set, then lift on to a cooling rack.

Melt the chocolate (page 10). Spread over the smooth sides of the biscuits. Before it sets, mark in wavy lines with the prongs of a fork.

Makes about 8

Devil's Food Cake

Undoubtedly one of America's best-known cakes for which there are countless recipes. Yet few things are more tempting than the sight of a slice of rich dark chocolate cake filled and topped with thick white frosting – Devil's Food Cake is a very apt name.

150 ml/¼ pint milk
225 g/8 oz soft brown sugar
50 g/2 oz cocoa powder
100 g/4 oz butter
2 eggs, beaten
225 g/8 oz plain flour
1 × 5 ml spoon/1 teaspoon bicarbonate of soda

FROSTING

450 g/1 lb granulated sugar
150 ml/¼ pint water
2 egg whites

Grease and line a 20 cm/8 inch cake tin. Put the milk, sugar, cocoa and butter in a pan. Heat gently, stirring until melted and smooth. Leave to cool. Beat in the eggs until smooth. Sift together the flour with the bicarbonate of soda and beat into the chocolate mixture to give a smooth thick batter.

Pour the batter into the prepared tin and bake in a warm oven, 160°C/325°F/Gas 3, for about 1 hour until risen and firm. Allow to cool in the tin for 5 minutes, then turn out on to a wire rack and leave to cool. When cold, split into three rounds.

To make the frosting, put the sugar and water in a small pan. Stir over low heat to dissolve the sugar, then boil to 115°C/240°F on a sugar thermometer (soft ball stage). Whisk the egg whites in a large mixing bowl until very stiff. When the syrup has reached the required temperature, allow the bubbles to subside, then pour on to the whisked egg whites, whisking all the time. Continue whisking until the frosting thickens and stands in soft peaks. Use at once to sandwich together the rounds of cake. Spread the remaining frosting over the cake, swirling with a palette knife and pulling up into peaks. Leave to set for 30 minutes.

Dobos Torte

The distinctive part about Hungary's most famous cake is the caramel spread over the top of it. This not only makes it look very attractive, but also adds a subtle flavour.

4 eggs, separated

125 g / 5 oz caster sugar

100 g / 4 oz ground hazelnuts (see **Note**)

FILLING

100 g / 4 oz plain chocolate,
broken into pieces

100 g / 4 oz unsalted butter

50 g / 2 oz icing sugar, sifted

TOPPING

75 g / 3 oz granulated **or** lump sugar

3 × 15 ml spoons / 3 tablespoons water

a few whole hazelnuts

Grease and line two 17.5 cm / 7 inch sandwich tins, preferably with non-stick silicone paper. Whisk the egg yolks and sugar until thick and creamy. Whisk the egg whites until they form stiff peaks. Fold the hazelnuts and egg whites alternately into the egg yolks.

Divide the mixture between the two tins and bake in a moderate oven, 180°C/350°F/Gas 4, for 30 minutes or until set. Allow to cool in the tins for 10 minutes, then turn out on to a wire rack and leave to cool.

To make the filling, melt the chocolate (page 10). Cream the butter and icing sugar, then beat in the chocolate. Use half of the mixture to sandwich together the two cakes.

To make the topping, put the sugar and water into a small pan and stir over low heat until the sugar has dissolved. Bring to the boil and boil rapidly to 176°C/345°F on a sugar thermometer (caramel stage). Using an oiled knife, spread the caramel evenly over the top of the cake. While it is still soft, mark into eight portions with a sharp knife and leave to set.

Put the remaining butter icing into a piping bag and pipe round the edge of the cake. Decorate with a few whole hazelnuts.

Note   *Ready ground hazelnuts may be used, or, if preferred, whole hazelnuts may be ground in a blender or food processor.*

Schwarzwälderkirschtorte

This classic German gâteau, known in translation as Black Forest Cherry Gâteau, should be made with Morello cherries, but their season is fairly short, and even in summer they are not readily available. I have, therefore, suggested using frozen pitted cherries which can be found in many supermarkets and most deep-freeze centres.

5 eggs
150 g / 5 oz caster sugar
100 g / 4 oz self-raising flour
25 g / 1 oz cocoa powder
4 × 15 ml spoons / 4 tablespoons vegetable oil

FILLING AND DECORATION

450 g / 1 lb frozen pitted black cherries, thawed
6 × 15 ml spoons / 6 tablespoons Kirsch
450 ml / ¾ pint double cream
50 g / 2 oz icing sugar, sifted
50 g / 2 oz plain chocolate caraque (page 12)

Grease and line a 22.5 cm/9 inch round cake tin. Whisk the eggs and sugar until thick and creamy, and the whisk leaves a trail when lifted out of the mixture. Sift in the flour and cocoa and fold into the mixture. Fold in the oil.

Turn the mixture into the prepared tin and bake in a moderately hot oven, 190°C/357°F/Gas 5, for about 30 minutes. Allow to cool in the tin for 5 minutes, then turn out on to a wire rack and leave to cool.

To make the filling and decoration, drain the juice from the cherries into a small pan, bring to the boil and boil rapidly until only about 2 × 15 ml spoons/ 2 tablespoons of syrup are left. Remove from the heat and stir in the cherries and half the Kirsch. Whip the cream until it holds its shape, then fold in the remaining Kirsch and the icing sugar.

Split the cake into three rounds. Place the bottom round on a serving plate, spread with some of the cream and half the cherries, place the second round on top, spread with more cream and the rest of the cherries, and then top with the last round. Spread the remaining cream over the cake, bringing it up into swirls. Decorate the top with the chocolate caraque and chill until ready to serve.

American Chocolate Mousse Torte

This is a somewhat unusual recipe. Three-quarters of the mixture is first baked; this rises rather like a soufflé, and then sinks in the middle as it cools. The hole in the centre is then filled with the remainder of the uncooked mixture.

2 × 15 ml spoons / 2 tablespoons dry breadcrumbs (raspings)
225 g / 8 oz plain chocolate, broken into pieces
1 × 15 ml spoon / 1 tablespoon instant coffee granules
4 × 15 ml spoons / 4 tablespoons water
8 eggs, separated
175 g / 6 oz caster sugar
1 × 5 ml spoon / 1 teaspoon vanilla essence

DECORATION

150 ml / ¼ pint whipping cream
chocolate curls (page 12)

Lightly butter a 22.5 cm/9 inch flan dish or tin (approximately 1.2 litre/2 pint capacity) and coat with the dry breadcrumbs. Melt the chocolate with the coffee and water (page 10). Remove from the heat. Whisk together the egg yolks, sugar and vanilla essence in a large bowl until thick and creamy, then beat in the chocolate. Whisk the egg whites until stiff, then fold into the chocolate mixture. Fill the flan dish with about three-quarters of the mixture. Cover the remainder and chill in a refrigerator.

Bake the flan in a moderate oven, 180°C/350°F/ Gas 4, for 25 minutes. Turn off the oven and leave for a further 5 minutes, then remove and leave to cool for 2 hours.

Fill the cavity in the centre with the chilled mixture and chill in a refrigerator for 30 minutes. Whip the cream until stiff and spread over the top. Decorate with the chocolate curls.

Serves 6–8

Sacher Torte

Although this cake is named after the founder of the world-renowned Hotel Sacher in Vienna, the original recipe is generally regarded as quite secret.

225 g/8 oz plain chocolate,
broken into pieces

1 × 15 ml spoon/1 tablespoon strong
black coffee

225 g/8 oz butter

225 g/8 oz sugar

5 eggs, separated

175 g/6 oz self-raising flour, sifted

FILLING

4 × 15 ml spoons/4 tablespoons
apricot jam, sieved

ICING

175 g/6 oz plain chocolate,
broken into pieces

5 × 15 ml spoons/5 tablespoons strong
black coffee

175 g/6 oz icing sugar, sifted

Grease and line a 22.5 cm/9 inch cake tin. Melt the chocolate with the coffee (page 10) and allow to cool. Cream the butter and sugar until light and fluffy. Beat in the egg yolks, one at a time, then the cooled chocolate. Fold in the flour. Whisk the egg whites until they form stiff peaks, then fold gently into the mixture.

Turn the mixture into the prepared tin and bake in a cool oven, 150°C/300°F/Gas 2, for 1½ hours. Leave to cool in the tin for 15 minutes, then turn out on to a wire rack and leave to cool. When quite cold, split the cake into two rounds.

To make the filling, warm the apricot jam gently. Spread one round of the cake with most of the apricot jam, sandwich the rounds together, then brush the remainder of the apricot jam all over the cake.

To make the icing, melt the chocolate with the coffee (page 10). Remove from the heat and beat in the icing sugar. Pour the icing over the cake, spreading it evenly with a palette knife dipped in warm water. Leave to set for at least 1 hour. Serve with whipped cream.

Chocolate Eclairs

A simple and well-known chocolate classic.

65 g / 2½ oz plain flour
a pinch of salt
50 g / 2 oz butter, cut into small pieces
150 ml / ¼ pint water
2 eggs
1 egg yolk

FILLING AND ICING
300 ml / ½ pint double cream
1 egg white
1 × 15 ml spoon / 1 tablespoon icing sugar
175 g / 6 oz plain chocolate,
broken into pieces

Sift together the flour and salt on to a sheet of greaseproof paper. Put the butter into a pan with the water. Put over gentle heat until the butter has melted, then bring to the boil. Remove the pan from the heat, add the flour all at once and beat well until the mixture forms a soft ball and leaves the sides of the pan clean. If necessary, replace the pan over very low heat. Allow to cool slightly, then beat in the whole eggs and the egg yolk, one at a time, until a very smooth, shiny mixture results.

Put the pastry into a piping bag fitted with a 1.25 cm / ½ inch plain nozzle and pipe out 7.5 cm / 3 inch lengths on to greased baking trays; allow plenty of room on the trays for the éclairs to rise and spread.

Bake the éclairs in a moderately hot oven, 200°C / 400°F / Gas 6 for about 25 minutes, or until golden-brown. Remove from the oven, make a couple of slits in the sides of each one to allow the steam to escape and return to the oven for a further 5–10 minutes to dry out. Remove from the oven and leave to cool on a wire rack.

To make the filling, whip the cream until stiff. Whisk the egg white until it forms stiff peaks, then whisk in the icing sugar, 1 × 5 ml spoon / 1 teaspoon at a time. Fold into the cream. Make a slit down the side of each éclair and fill with the cream, or pipe it in.

Melt the chocolate (page 10), then pour into a container long enough to be able to dip the top surface of each éclair into the chocolate. Dip the tops of the éclairs into the chocolate, then leave to set.

Makes about 12

Bûche de Noel

France's classic Christmas cake – it freezes well so you can make it several weeks in advance.

4 eggs
100 g / 4 oz caster sugar
75 g / 3 oz self-raising flour
25 g / 1 oz cocoa powder
FILING AND ICING
150 ml / ¼ pint milk
2 egg yolks
175 g / 6 oz plain chocolate, broken into small pieces
100 g / 4 oz unsalted butter
50g / 2 oz icing sugar, sifted
extra icing sugar
holly **or** *other Christmas cake decorations*

Grease and line a 32.5 × 22.5 cm/13 × 9 inch Swiss roll tin. Whisk the eggs and sugar together until thick and creamy, and the whisk leaves a trail when lifted out of the mixture. Sift in the flour and cocoa, and fold in. Turn the mixture into the prepared tin.

Bake in a moderately hot oven, 200°C/400°F/Gas 6, for 12–15 minutes or until the cake springs back when pressed lightly. Turn out on to a piece of greaseproof or non-stick silicone paper dredged with icing or caster sugar. Carefully peel off the lining paper, trim off the edges, and roll up the Swiss roll, keeping the paper inside the roll. Put to one side and allow to cool.

To make the filling, heat the milk to blood temperature in a small saucepan. Blend the egg yolks in a basin or the top of a double saucepan, and beat in the milk. Stand the mixture over a pan of gently simmering water, and cook, stirring frequently, until the mixture coats the back of a wooden spoon. Add the chocolate, and stir until it has melted, then remove from the heat. Cover the basin with a piece of clingfilm and leave to cool, stirring from time to time. Cream the butter and beat in the icing sugar, then gradually beat in the cooled custard.

Unroll the Swiss roll, and spread with a third of the filling. Re-roll and spread the outside of the roll with the remaining icing.

Using a fork, mark lines on the top of the log, as if for the bark of a tree. Chill in a refrigerator for about 1 hour until set, then sprinkle all over with icing sugar, and decorate with holly, cake decorations, etc.

Chocolate Chiffon Pie

The Americans make a number of chiffon pies of which chocolate and lemon are the best known.

75 g/6 oz plain flour

a pinch of salt

75 g/3 oz butter **or** margarine

cold water

FILLING AND TOPPING

2 × 5 ml spoons/2 teaspoons
powdered gelatine

2 × 15 ml spoons/2 tablespoons cold water

3 eggs, separated

50 g/2 oz caster sugar

100 g/4 oz plain chocolate cake covering,
broken into pieces

1 × 15 ml spoon/1 tablespoon cocoa powder

1 × 5 ml spoon/1 teaspoon instant
coffee granules

150 ml/¼ pint whipping cream

Sift together the flour and salt. Rub in the butter or margarine until the mixture resembles fine breadcrumbs, then bind with cold water to make a firm dough. Turn on to a floured surface and knead lightly. Roll out and use to line a 20 cm/8 inch pie plate or dish. Bake blind in a moderately hot oven, 190°C/375°F/Gas 5, for 20–25 minutes. Leave to cool.

To make the filling, sprinkle the gelatine over the cold water in a basin. Leave to soften for 5 minutes. Put the egg yolks and sugar into the top of a double boiler or a basin over a pan of boiling water, and whisk until the mixture thickens. Whisk in the gelatine and stir until dissolved. Stir in the chocolate, cocoa and coffee granules. Continue stirring until the chocolate has melted. Remove from the heat and allow to cool slightly. Whisk the egg whites until they form stiff peaks, then fold into the chocolate mixture.

Turn the mixture into the baked flan case and chill in a refrigerator for at least 1 hour. Before serving, whip the cream lightly, and spread over the top of the pie.

Serves 4–6

Nègre en Chemise

A superb French recipe, Nègre en Chemise is a very sophisticated steamed pudding.

100g/4oz sliced white bread,
crusts removed

150ml/¼ pint double cream

50g/2oz plain chocolate, broken into pieces

100g/4oz butter

50g/2oz ground almonds

75g/3oz caster sugar

4 eggs, each beaten separately

150ml/¼ pint whipping cream

15g/½oz icing sugar, sifted

Well butter a 1.2 litre/2 pint mould or pudding basin. Put the bread into a shallow dish and pour over the cream. Leave for about 10 minutes, then mash with a fork. Melt the chocolate (page 10). Cream the butter, then, either by hand or, preferably, using an electric beater, beat in the bread, almonds, sugar and chocolate, and continue beating until the mixture is smooth. Beat in the eggs, one at a time.

Turn the mixture into the prepared mould or basin. Cover with a double layer of buttered greaseproof paper or with foil, and steam for 1½–2 hours (add more boiling water to the pan if necessary).

Whip the cream until stiff and sweeten with the icing sugar. Turn the pudding out of the mould or basin and serve immediately with the cream.

Serves 6

La Dame Blanche

Found on the menu of every Luxembourg restaurant, this recipe is sometimes made without the meringue shells.

300ml/½ pint vanilla ice cream

4 meringue shells

cold Rich Chocolate Sauce (1) (page 89)

CRÈME CHANTILLY

150ml/¼ pint double cream

1 egg white

1 × 15ml spoon/1 tablespoon
icing sugar, sifted

Make the crème chantilly first. Whip the cream until it holds its shape. Whisk the egg white until stiff, then whisk in the icing sugar, 1 × 5ml spoon/ 1 teaspoon at a time. Fold into the cream.

Put two scoops of the ice cream on each serving plate. Top with a meringue shell, then pour over a quarter of the chocolate sauce and top with a quarter of the crème chantilly. Serve at once.

Serves 4

Pots au Chocolat

A wonderful chocolate mousse recipe given to me by a friend in Fife. Her pots au chocolat were so popular throughout Fife that she could never give a dinner party without serving them. They also freeze extremely well, so it is worth making a double quantity and freezing half.

1 fat vanilla pod
225 g/8 oz plain chocolate, broken into pieces
1 × 15 ml spoon/1 tablespoon icing sugar
25 g/1 oz butter
3 egg yolks
300 ml/½ pint double cream

DECORATION
25 g/1 oz flaked almonds

Using a pointed, sharp knife, split open the vanilla pod and, with a small spoon, scrape out all the moist inside. Melt the chocolate with the icing sugar, butter and the inside of the vanilla pod (page 10). Remove from the heat and beat in the egg yolks. Whip the cream until it holds its shape, then beat in the chocolate mixture and whisk until thick. Turn into six small ramekins and sprinkle with the almonds. Chill in a refrigerator until ready to serve.

Serves 6

Saint Emilion au Chocolat

A classic French recipe and a simple way of producing a really elegant dessert.

12–16 macaroons
4 × 15 ml spoons/4 tablespoons dark rum
100 g/4 oz butter
100 g/4 oz caster sugar
150 ml/¼ pint milk
1 egg
225 g/8 oz plain chocolate, broken into pieces

Put the macaroons on to a flat dish and sprinkle lightly with the rum. Cream together the butter and sugar until light and fluffy. Put the milk into a pan and bring to the boil. Remove from the heat, leave for about 10 minutes to cool, then beat in the egg.

Melt the chocolate (page 10) and, leaving it over the heat, beat in the milk, then the butter and sugar. Continue to beat until very smooth.

Put four of the macaroons into the bottom of a serving dish. Pour over half the chocolate sauce. Repeat with four more macaroons and the rest of the chocolate sauce. Top with the remaining macaroons. Chill in a refrigerator for at least 12 hours.

Serves 6–8

Chocolate and Pineapple Roulade

A roulade really is the ultimate 'Swiss roll' – a cake, but without any flour. I have tried making it both with cocoa and with melted chocolate, and, perhaps surprisingly, prefer a cocoa-based one.

4 eggs, separated
125 g / 5 oz caster sugar
1 × 1.25 ml spoon / ¼ teaspoon vanilla essence
40 g / 1½ oz cocoa powder

FILLING AND DECORATION

300 ml / ½ pint double cream
*450 g / 1 lb pineapple pieces, fresh **or** canned and drained*
chocolate vermicelli

Grease and line a 32.5 × 22.5 cm / 13 × 9 inch Swiss roll tin. Whisk the egg yolks, sugar and vanilla essence until thick and creamy. Whisk the egg whites until they form stiff peaks. Fold the cocoa into the egg yolks. Stir in 1 × 15 ml spoon / 1 tablespoon of the whisked egg white. Fold in the remainder of the egg white.

Turn the mixture into the prepared tin and spread evenly. Bake in a moderate oven, 180°C / 350°F / Gas 4, for 15 minutes or until just cooked. Do not overcook or the roll will crack more easily. Remove from the oven, cover with a clean tea-towel and leave until quite cold. Invert on to a piece of greaseproof paper dredged with caster sugar, and peel off the paper carefully.

To make the filling, whip the cream until stiff. Reserve a few pieces of the pineapple for decoration and mix the remaining pineapple with two-thirds of the cream. Spread evenly all over the roulade, then roll it up, pushing it along the greaseproof paper. Place on a serving dish. Pipe the remaining cream along the top to decorate, and top with the remaining pieces of pineapple and the chocolate vermicelli.

Serves 6–8

Note *Do not worry if the roulade cracks slightly when you roll it up as you can always mask the cracks with cream or sprinkle icing sugar over them.*

Bavarois au Chocolat

Moulded desserts were particularly popular during Queen Victoria's reign. A Victorian style china mould will create a truly authentic looking dessert.

15 g / ½ oz powdered gelatine
4 × 15 ml spoons / 4 tablespoons cold water
4 egg yolks
50 g / 2 oz caster sugar
1 × 5 ml spoon / 1 teaspoon vanilla essence
600 ml / 1 pint milk
225 g / 8 oz plain chocolate, broken into small pieces
150 ml / ¼ pint double cream
150 ml / ¼ pint single cream

DECORATION
chocolate curls (page 12) **or** *whipped cream*

Oil a 1.5 litre / 2½ pint mould lightly or dampen with cold water. Sprinkle the gelatine over the water in a basin and leave to soften for about 5 minutes. Beat together the egg yolks, sugar and vanilla essence for 5 minutes. Warm the milk and stir into the egg yolks and sugar. Blend well and put into the top of a double saucepan, or into a bowl placed over a pan of gently simmering water. Cook gently, stirring all the time, until the mixture thickens. Stir in the softened gelatine and, when this has dissolved, add the chocolate. Stir until the chocolate has melted. Remove from the heat, put into a cold place and leave until the mixture begins to thicken. Whip the double and single creams lightly and fold into the mixture when it is thick but not set. Turn into the prepared mould and chill for at least 2 hours or until set.

To turn out, dip the mould into boiling water (see Note). Invert on to a plate and remove the mould. Decorate with chocolate curls or whipped cream.

Serves 6–8

Note *If using a tin mould, dip for 3–4 seconds. If using a china mould, about 15 seconds will be required.*

Index